SOCIETYSPECTACLE

ISBN (print): 978-1-916541-24-5
ISBN (ebook): 978-1-916541-25-2

First edition.

First published in 2026 by Erratum Press
Sheffield, UK
www.erratumpress.com

Design and typesetting by Ansgar Allen

SOCIETYSPECTACLE

the Eye in Don DeLillo

Grant Maierhofer

ERRATUM PRESS
ACADEMIC DIVISION

for my family
and for Don DeLillo

[1]

Because it is, to me, an utterly ideal means of accounting for the whole of DeLillo's body of work tidily, I am only consciously stealing an aspect of Michael Naas's superlative works on the author. I can say this, because I have only read this portion of Naas's books, not allowing myself to consult anything else until this book is finished, and when it is finished, in August of 2025, I'll buy both of them and read them in their entirety. Naas's approach to their titles is, to me, perfect, and that is, in turn, how I'll be referring to them. Thank you, then, to Mr. Naas, for this, and with that I heartily recommend checking out his books, in particular the DeLillos, as I'm quite certain the remainder of their contents is equally inspired.

I'd also like to note that, while initially I'd thought it seemed somehow more meaningful to consider the whole of DeLillo's output, i.e. the plays, all the stories, any nonfiction, anything, I no longer feel that way. DeLillo's great concern has seemed to me to be the novel, i.e. the Novel, as a form, and as a means of expressing and exploring dimensions of our world, and thus I'm only listing those works to which I'm giving any, however scant, attention I've got.

1 "The Triumph of Death," by Pieter Bruegel the Elder.

A, *Americana*—DeLillo, Don. *Americana.* Reissued. London: Penguin books, 2013.

EZ, *End Zone*—DeLillo, Don. *End Zone.* Boston: Houghton Mifflin Company, 1972.

GJS, *Great Jones Street*—DeLillo, Don. *Great Jones Street.* Boston: Houghton Mifflin Company, 1973.

RS, *Ratner's Star*—DeLillo, Don. *Ratner's Star.* 1st Vintage Books ed. New York: Vintage Books, 1980.

P, *Players*—DeLillo, Don. *Players.* First edition. New York: Alfred A. Knopf, 1977.

RD, *Running Dog*—DeLillo, Don. Running Dog. First edition. New York: Alfred A. Knopf, 1978.

(I will not be consulting *Amazons* as I gave my copy to the woman who manages our ice rink.)

TN, *The Names*—DeLillo, Don. Don DeLillo: Three Novels of the 1980s : *The Names ; White Noise ; Libra.* Vol. 363. New York, N.Y: The Library of America, 2022.

L, *Libra*—Ibid.

WN, *White Noise*—Ibid.

MII, *Mao II*—DeLillo, Don, and Don DeLillo. *Mao II ; Underworld.* Edited by Mark Osteen. New York, N.Y: The Library of America, 2023.

U, *Underworld*—Ibid.

TBA, *The Body Artist*—DeLillo, Don. *The Body Artist* : A Novel. New York: Scribner, 2001.

C, *Cosmopolis*—DeLillo, Don. *Cosmopolis*: A Novel. Scribner trade pbk. ed. New York: Scribner, 2012.

FM, *Falling Man*—DeLillo, Don. Falling Man : A Novel. First Scribner hardcover edition. New York: Scribner, 2007.

PM, *Point Omega*—DeLillo, Don. Point Omega : A Novel. First Scribner hardcover edition. New York: Scribner, 2010.

ZK, *Zero K*—DeLillo, Don. Zero K : A Novel. First Scribner hardcover edition. New York: Scribner, 2016.

TS, *The Silence*—DeLillo, Don. The Silence. New York, New York: Scribner, 2020.

Stories:

BM, "Baader-Meinhof"— DeLillo, Don. *Baader-Meinhof. The New Yorker.* Vol. 78. New York: Condé Nast Publications, Inc, 2002.

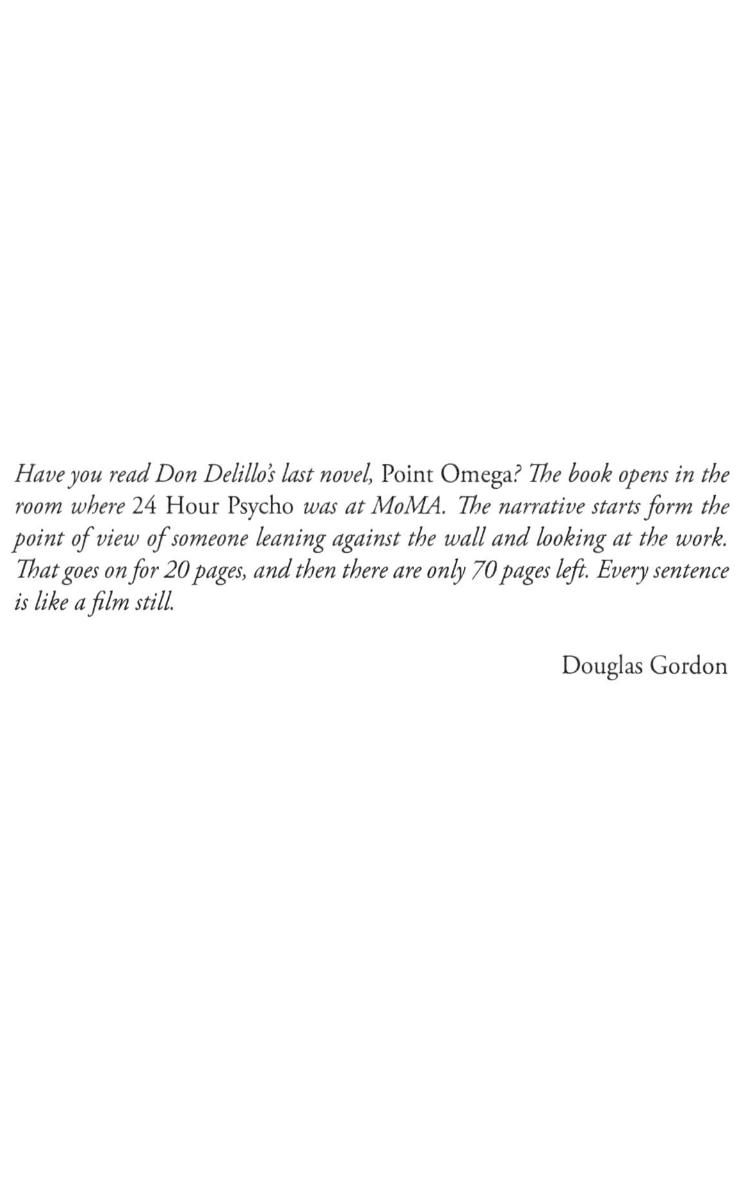

Have you read Don Delillo's last novel, Point Omega*? The book opens in the room where* 24 Hour Psycho *was at MoMA. The narrative starts form the point of view of someone leaning against the wall and looking at the work. That goes on for 20 pages, and then there are only 70 pages left. Every sentence is like a film still.*

Douglas Gordon

👁 👁 WHAT DOES THE AMERICAN NOVELIST (WRITER) DON DELILLO HAVE TO TELL ME ABOUT EYEBALLS? WHAT DOES DON DELILLO HAVE TO TELL ME ABOUT THE EYE AND THE MAKING OF FICTIONAL LITERATURE? WHAT DOES GUY DEBORD HAVE TO TELL ME ABOUT CRITICISM? WHAT DO EITHER OF THESE FIGURES HAVE TO DO WITH ACADEMIC WORK? WHAT, IF ANYTHING, IS THE WORTH OF ACADEMIC WORK? WHAT IS AN ACADEMIC? WHAT IS AN IMAGE, IN FICTION? WHAT IS SEEING, IN A FICTIONAL NOVEL? HOW DOES THE INFLUENCE OF THE IMAGE PLAY OUT IN THE WORK OF WRITER? WHAT, IF ANY, IS THE FUNCTION OF A WORK EXACTLY LIKE THIS (THOUGH POTENTIALLY NOT THIS) WHEN WRITTEN, ASSEMBLED, PUBLISHED?

👁 👁 In societies where modern conditions of the production of fiction, of literature, prevail, all of life presents itself as an immense accumulation of spectacles, i.e., *compel me, entertain me, entice me, comfort and critique me, or certainly I will die.* Everything that was directly lived, i.e. experienced, messy, ugly, human, flawed yet vying, has moved away into a representation.[2]

[2] This is the first of several reworkings of sections of Guy Debord's *The Society of the Spectacle*, which is used as a kind of lens to give this work a firmer shape.

◉ ◉ THE WRITER ON SPECTACLE: "Maybe it is the evanescent spectacle of contemporary life that makes the novel so nervous. Things flash and die. A face appears, a movie actor's, say, and it seems to be everywhere, suddenly; or it is an entire movie that's everywhere, with enormous feature stories about special effects and global marketing and tie-in merchandise; or it is just an individual's name that haunts every informational nook, and you can't figure out who the person is inside the name or what the context is that gave such abrupt prominence to the name, but it never actually matters and this is the point."[3]

3 DeLillo, Don, *The Power of History*: https://archive.nytimes.com/www.nytimes.com/library/books/090797article3.html

👁 👁 This is the point. The scattered brain is the point. Both the scattered brain on Zapruder's film and the scattered brain of modern consciousness—i.e., consciousness since WWII, which only grew insanely more scattered in the image-richness of the 1960s, with images of burning monks, burned and stripped Vietnamese children, flower children, Woodstock, police violence, and a growing lack of trust in their language, favoring instead these images, these signs, the icons, these symbols. The nervousness of the novel in this case refers to *Underworld*, but of course it refers—can refer—to the entirety of his output. They're all nervous, frenetic, jagged, overwhelmed by modern consciousness. He is discussing, Writer is—sometimes herein referred to as DeLillo, probably more often referred to as Writer—the weird amalgam that led to *Underworld's* genesis, the middle-ish-career tome, that elucidates both forwards and backwards all of his career. Two headlines in a newspaper: one recounting "The Shot Heard 'Round the World," when Bobby Thomson hits a game-winning home run, the 40th anniversary of same, and one informing the populace that the Soviets had successfully detonated an atomic bomb. The Writer sees these twinned polarities and burrows into them, extracting something that feels somehow like history and more; contemporary history as Herodotus might've written it, as Thucydides did, with great invention, recount the trajectory of the Peloponnesian War. He is demonstrating the process that has served him now for decades, taken him from the Old World ruins of Greece to Dallas, Texas on November 22, 1963, taken him throughout the realms of college football, academia, family life, rock 'n' roll celebrity burnout, and the paranoiac obsession with footage from Hitler's bunker. He offers little in the way of quotation, and notably—given the contours of this particular text—cites the painter Willem de Kooning when discussing the notion of American work he's trying—has tried—as a writer to process: "It's a certain burden, this Americanness. If you come from a small nation, you don't have that. … I feel sometimes an American artist must feel like a baseball player or something — a member of a team writing American history." Writer goes on: "Novelists don't feel like team members. But the sweeping range of American landscape and experience can be a goad, a challenge, an affliction and an inspiration, pretty much in one package." He discusses, in the closing of this piece, published in the New York Time Book Review in support of *Underworld*, the further unique ways in which the image—i.e. *the eye*, what it sees—has guided him: "You're watching a video-tape of hooded men emerging from a bank and they move with a certain choreographed flair, firing virtuoso bursts from automatic weapons, and you wonder if they are repeating a scene from a recent movie, the one that disappeared overnight when the weekend gross was flat, and the tape is played and replayed, exhausting all the reality stored in its magnetic pores," […] "Or you're staring at the inside of a convenience store on a humdrum night in July. This is a surveillance video with a digital display that marks off the tenths of seconds. Then you see a shuffling man with a handgun enter the frame. The commonplace homicide that ensues is transformed in the image-act of your own witness. It is bare, it is real, it is live, it is taped. It is compelling, it is numbing, it is digitally microtimed and therefore filled with incessant information. And if you view the tape enough, it tends to transform you, to make you a passive variation of the armed robber in his warped act of consumption. It is another set of images for you to want and need and get sick of and need nonetheless, and it separates you from the reality that beats ever more softly in the diminishing world outside the tape." […] "Against these flashes, these lonely fleeting images, against the ritual arrangement of these serial replays, events and documents of the past have a clarity and intactness that amount to a moral burnish. A Matthew Brady photograph, a framed front page—'Men Walk on the Moon.' These things represent moments of binding power. They draw people together in ways that only the most disastrous contemporary events can match. We depend on disaster to consolidate our vision." To repeat, then, our altered Debord: In societies where modern conditions of the production of fiction, of literature, prevail, all of life presents itself as an immense accumulation of spectacles, i.e., *compel me, entertain me, entice me, comfort and critique me, or certainly I will die*. Everything that was directly lived, i.e. experienced, messy, ugly, human, flawed yet vying, has moved away into a representation. We return, then, to the first proper iteration of Writer's method—excepting several short stories—these factors at work in *Americana* (1971).

👁 👁 THE EYE AND THE SPECTACLE IN *AMERICANA*: "The war was on television every night but we all went to the movies. Soon most of the movies began to look alike and we went into dim rooms and turned on or off, or watched others turn on or off, or burned joss sticks and listened to tapes of near silence. Then we invented the anti-orgies. (These were touchless events by and large, perhaps inspired, ultimately, by film clips of the uninterrupted war—full circle for technotronic man.) There were about half a dozen such events that year and almost immediately they became as predictable as the movies. So we made movies of the anti-orgies. I brought my 16mm camera along. It was a witty toy and everyone was delighted, maybe because it made touchlessness less decadent. The six or seven people in attendance—an odd number was preferable—seemed much more interested in the camera than in the coy satyricons for which we had assembled. The camera released people. It lifted some hopelessly cornered shadow out of their dreams and the two elements struggled to merge, the negative and the final print, image and self, in the shock of banked lights. Their images were in my camera, swimming among the silver halide crystals suspended in gelatin, while they themselves tried to drift toward that moment, lost in dust and mist, when Africa was rising. The participants danced for the camera, never man and woman however, always separately, creating preposterous dream ballets that seemed intended to express the chants and fires of an identity discovered as joyously as a continent. Warrior drums beat from the stereo and in the circles of my right eye I received the spectacle."

A, 5-6

👁 👁 Though published novels prior to 1971 in America or anywhere certainly attempted to reckon with the reality of technology, there's a slippery aspect to this that makes it feel unique in that camp. It isn't taking a position, necessarily, or if it is it's taking the position of the status quo—its narrator, David Bell, is a semi-likable cipher who, like Nick Carraway, functions best as an observer of the world, intermittently cheering it on or relishing its cliches and his clichedom, but eluding firm standing as a conventional fictive protagonist because he's always fixated on the world—and the status quo of the 1970s is wet with imagery, dense with it in every respect, and people are relating now to the movies, to seeing themselves filmed, to seeing themselves on screen, to seeing the camera itself, and it is burrowing into them. "The camera released people. It lifted some hopelessly cornered shadow out of their dreams and the two elements struggled to merge, the negative and the final print, image and self, in the shock of banked lights." Prior to this the notion of encountering such language in a novel not set in Hollywood would seem ludicrous. This is, however, a world encountering tidal shifts in almost every respect. Bell isn't simply a cipher, then, but a kind of test subject for the struggles of his age. He stands between these primitive images, these social impulses, and the apparent freedom of the world of the eye, the performative space of celluloid.

👁 👁 The first novel of any writer—or at the least the first *published* novel, though even this isn't universal (T. Wolff, for example)—is forever tied to their eventual output, its DNA. In some cases, in fact very probably in most cases, the first novel is something to be vanquished by the later work. In DeLillo's case, hereinafter most often referred to as Writer, for simplicity's sake, there are ways in which what follows does effectively vanquish *Americana*, and yet his preoccupations are all there; and probably most importantly, his language is all there. In Writer's work, the language is the thing. Other novelists had certainly embodied this prior to Writer—Stein, Joyce, arguably Melville quite often, to name just a few who wrote in English—but DeLillo advances this notion of the Language as the Thing for a writer of fiction to a place you can think of as Wittgensteinian. The language makes his worlds, and it is from the language—the language only—that each of his books, *Americana* included, gets constructed.

👁 👁 That we are saturated in the image is not news.[4] That this generation, or any living generation—I was born in 1990—have lived saturated in the image is not news, is not revealing. I have tried, in my life, to find how anyone *after* the television, the film, might attempt to write anything at all; let alone novels, let alone publish them, let alone have them read, let alone do anything interesting in them. I have looked into the lives of writers to find some reflection of myself, perhaps, my thoughts, my hopes, my pathetic ambitions, my TV watching habits, my antidepressant medications, my identity as a parent. I have sought this because the life of someone writing is a lonely life, which is not the same thing exactly as the person who happens to be that "someone" "writing". What I mean to say is that the particular act of writing something, when one is pushing oneself in the way one ought to push oneself, is a lonely, fearful, odd experience. Almost all of the artists I've looked at do some version of this, then; they post pictures of their kin to the insides of their lockers, as it were. Don DeLillo—or, the Writer, or Writer—is not, then, the end-all-be-all for our writers, or our readers, or for me. What he is is the most successful literary artist of a particular type I've encountered in my lifetime. What I mean by this has nothing to do with money. What I mean by this is that DeLillo, the Writer, has realized a vision that has in turn been made commensurate with the goals of the writer, i.e. that someone, anyone, somewhere, anywhere, *reads* their stuff, in a manner befitting their vision for said stuff, without sacrificing or kowtowing endlessly, or simply slapping the reader in the face with their genius, and moving on indifferently. I believe that he is the great excavator of the Image in fiction, a master of the Eye, and I believe too that the Image, and with it the video, the film, is one of if not the greatest problem(s) of the twentieth and early twenty-first century, one of our most important considerations, and thus I assign a great deal of weight to DeLillo's project. What's more, it's not as if he's shied from images of a particular weight. Quite the opposite:

4 "The images detached from every aspect of life fuse in a common stream in which the unity of this life can no longer be reestablished. Reality considered partially unfolds, in its own general unity, as a pseudo-world apart, an object of mere contemplation. The specialization of images of the world is completed in the world of the autonomous image, where the liar has lied to himself. The spectacle in general, as the concrete inversion of life, is the autonomous movement of the non-living." (Debord, *Society of the Spectacle*)

when the "Falling Man"[5] photograph is circulated, immediately the Writer seems to need to write a novel about it. When he writes of JFK, he does so via Abraham Zapruder's footage of his assassination, fixating on that bit of twentieth century video ephemera in a manner foretelling YouTube sleuths and Reddit obsessives. His subject matter, then, lines up as perfectly with his present as any writer's, and his relationship to it, to his present, is treated simultaneously with a high seriousness and an ironic remove that strikes me as infinitely useful to those wanting to figure their medium out. This is readily apparent when looking at those he's influenced—David Foster Wallace, Tracy O'Neill, Bret Easton Ellis, Chang-Rae Lee, and on and on and on. If Andy Warhol might be deemed the visual artist who most effectively regurgitated his present culture into the captivated eyeballs of his audience, then DeLillo appears to be his equivalent in prose.

5 "Richard Drew, *Falling Man*, 2001. Courtesy AP Photos.; After 9/11: Photography, the Destructive Sublime, and the Postmodern Archive." In the digital collection Michigan Quarterly Review Images. https://quod.lib.umich.edu/m/mqrimage/x-06201-und-03/06201_03. University of Michigan Library Digital nCollections. Accessed October 08, 2024.

The dominant narrative mode concerned itself with what it concerned itself with, as "all of society, as part of society, and as instrument of unification," (Debord) "As a part of society it is specifically the sector which concentrates all gazing and all consciousness," (Debord). The world became extremely concerned with seeing, with looking, with staring, with the electronic distribution of images, of text, of moving pictures and of News, twenty-four hours each day, building, building, since the first stories of the Writer are published in the 60s, and into the 1970s, from 1971, when *Americana* is published, and which closes with a man viewing the world with his home video camera, through to *The Silence*, his spare, monastic, ascetic novel wherein the screens and the electrical grid are all apocalyptically shut down during the Super Bowl. As society shifted the Writer shifted, and those seemingly on its edge became obsessive lookers, starers, oglers, watchers, and nobody's work was as suffused with this inclination as the Writer's.

👁 👁 THE SPECTACLE IN *END ZONE*: “Look, Gary, if I go out and talk to different groups about this sort of thing, it doesn’t make me some kind of monster who likes to expound or whatever the word is on the consequences of nuclear exchange, who likes to stand up there before a group and talk about mass death and all the rest of it. If I try to inform people so they’ll do something about the situation, the gravity of it, then I’m performing a service, or at least it seems to me. I’m not some kind of monstrous creature who enjoys talking about the spectacle of megadeath, the unprecedented scale of this kind of thing. It has to be talked about and expounded on. It has to be described for people, clinically and graphically, so they’ll know just what it is they’re facing.”

EZ, 85

◉ ◉ *End Zone* follows in 1972 and really is quite astounding for its significant departure from *Americana*. It lays, more or less, the remaining groundwork for what's to come in Writer's preoccupations. Adding in sport, in varying forms. Adding in the obsessive and meticulous nature of American institutions—in this case Logos College in West Texas. Adding in, further, this looming threat of the end of the world, i.e. death, in this case by way of a course on "modern warfare," and its protagonist's, Gary Harkness, fixation on the prospect of nuclear war. The voice remains Writer's, with its firm declarations on the nature of things, tendency to list, and fascination with the data of both college football and nuclear armament; but even this example illustrates that he's already found a new context which pushes back enough on this voice—admittedly a voice that can steer the ship so firmly, at times, as to feel almost alien; *too much*—to open up new pathways into modern consciousness and life.

👁 👁 I remember I was living in Chicago when I saw it advertised online that Writer was going to be presenting somewhere on the Zapruder film. I don't remember where it was going to be. I knew I couldn't go, but I hoped maybe I could find a video of it after he'd presented. To a certain extent, I almost think there was a video of it somewhere, once, but I can't find it. I could find the exact listing for it I'm sure, but that's not really what I'm getting at. I heard this, and thought about it, and seemed to settle into a new understanding of the writing of Writer. I'd been reading *Great Jones Street* while I rode the train to and from college, rereading over the lyrics of Bucky Wunderlich's band and trying to understand how they related to the rest of this paranoid work. First, when I'd lived in Minneapolis, I'd read *White Noise*, and going forward his work's importance grew and grew in my estimation—the sense that he was saying something essential, that I needed to encounter, and ingest, began and continued to loom over me. Another time, while I was reading *Mao II*, about to take the Amtrak back to snowbound Wisconsin, home for winter break—I wrote a bad novel, if memory serves—I put down the book for a minute and opened my phone. I'd received an email from the Art Institute in Chicago, Warhol's "Mao" paintings were going to be shown. I took it heavily, and dove back into my reading.[6] I pictured the room. I pictured Writer standing somewhere, holding a small clicker, playing through slides maybe. Talking over it. Talking about the bullet. Talking about the bullets. Talking too about Abraham Zapruder. The man's growing sense of it all, both Zapruder and Writer, really. Around this time, or at a maximum two or three years later, the artist Richard Prince posted a picture of Writer on Twitter. He stood in front of a painting someplace. He wore a simple shirt, either light blue or deep green, with I think dark blue khakis, and his sleeves rolled up. My sense of him grew then too. I don't know what happened to it. I don't believe it's anywhere now. I've attempted, multiple times, both to search Twitter, Richard Prince's Twitter, to find it. I've searched, too, via Wayback Machine, which lets you view old webpages. I've done this more than once. This aspect of reading, of study, of scholarship, is difficult to explain. It is difficult to explain how it is those things. It is, of course, an obsession. I remember hearing, on an episode of The Great Concavity's podcast, wherein they discussed the letters between David Foster Wallace and Writer. At one point, it's indicated that Wallace sort of came to regret becoming so close to Writer, since it seemed to have slightly

6 "The spectacle is not a collection of images, but a social relation among people, mediated by images." (Debord, *Society of the Spectacle*).

soured his initial sense of total idol worship one undergoes when finding a Writer who seems to embody an ideal we'd like ourselves to embody. I acknowledge this only to present the balance of this sort of thing. I've experienced what Wallace potentially experienced, mainly in the form of Writer's voice reading his works. I don't believe we always need to hear the work from every writer read aloud. In the case of Writer, something in his reading voice got so embedded that it can be quite difficult for me to separate the reading of his texts with that sound. What *End Zone* presents, then, is a way out of that sound, and when we consider the tendency so frequent in writers—to establish a voice and then hold to it like life itself—this seems quite significant. That image, too, of Writer, both in his presentation of Abraham Zapruder's footage, and standing before some work of his friend, Richard Prince, are such glowing things to me, such lively and incredible things—like Joyce's spirited engagement with his daughter, Lucia Joyce, at this horrendous moment when both of them were seemingly losing their sense of reality, and Nora wanted practicality, and stability, and a wedge existed between her and Lucia as a result—that they are now as much a part of my experience of the eye in Writer's work as his frankly otherworldly, Godlike, unbelievable dissection of *24 Hour Psycho* in *Point Omega*.

👁 👁 The concept of spectacle unifies most if not all of American literature of a certain stripe—angry, language-oriented, artful—in the years after the 1960s, when the notion of American literature had started to get relegated behind a more saturated and seemingly natural spectacle in American cinema—the two have, ever since, been grappling, often compellingly, with one another. The variety and the dissonance between these works cannot be overstated, i.e., they are all ingesting—witnessing—the same thing(s), but the manner in which each of them (really both the writers and the filmmakers, though herein primarily the writers, or rather the Writer) reacts to and renders it attests to a new kind of Emersonian Truth, a fictional reality unto itself, that Writer, more than most of them, has carved and carved with such determination as to seemingly almost leave the earthly plane. "Considered in its own terms, the spectacle is affirmation of appearance and affirmation of all human life, namely *social* life, as mere appearance. But the critique which reaches the truth of the spectacle exposes it as the visible negation of life, as a negation of life which has *become* visible." (Italics mine)[7]

[7] Partial reworking and quoting of (10.) Debord, *Society of the Spectacle.*

👁 👁 Writers, Writer told *Panic* in 2005, "must oppose things, oppose whatever power tries to impose on us," thus implying either a continuum on which all writers of necessity exist—it is the belief of the author of this text that this continuum does exist, from the crude scrawl of a child, say, to the entirely expert chess annotations of a Grand Master—or that the act of making fiction is one undertaken in opposition. To what, exactly? Writer says "power, corporations, the state, and the whole system of consumption and of debilitating entertainments" but really, in the spirit of total freedom in the making of anything—or not even the making of anything but the mere existence of anything, the anything of anything (there aren't rules)—one could safely hold that a writer is simply best off opposing something, anything, as a beginning. Per Debord, we get this strange spiraling back to Writer, wherein opposition—"critique" (granted, sure, not always opposition, sure, fine—that's fine)—can be the thing to "expose" the spectacle, the spectaclizing of daily life "as the visible negation of life," and "as a negation of life which has become visible," (Italics skipped) not unlike Writer's ingesting the world of America, "of Godard and Coca Cola," of advertising, of film, of New York City in the 1970s, a sight if ever there was one, and returning it to printed text, to words on a page, to subjective, rendered, highly interior language that does not appease, or ease, or merely tickle. It critiques, it *opposes*, it undoes in clean speech and sculptured letters one's propensity to nod—or, or at the very least it lets one progress (prompts one, even) in one's critiquing, one's beginning to looking askance; though it could not do this were it content to be merely in the tradition of The Novel, or Literature purely and simply, which one assumes is not enough.

👁 👁 This is also—if I say it is [Robert Rauschenberg *This Is a Portrait of Iris Clert If I Say So*, 1961]—a study of *reading*, as any work of criticism effectively is, whether on books or not, and especially when one considers the nature of the eye in DeLillo's corpus, the eye which pored over the Warren Commission Report is then affixed in abstracted shape to *Libra*, as is the eye reading the walls of the gallery in *Point Omega*, which we then can read—an adaptation of an adaptation of an adaptation of an adaptation of a work of writing, being written. I am interested in the nature of reading, of my own human relationship to the practice of reading, but also to the curious roles one occupies when one is writing a work to be read, about reading the work of another. I may be in the last dregs of students who saw the flickering lights going out of the MFA in America as a truly terminal degree—dwarfed as they currently are by Ph.D.s in the very same subjects—and thus there is a part of me that still stings when I admit, even in the back of my mind, that I never wrote a dissertation, that I don't necessarily have the bona fides of someone who had, and this kind of thing has doubtless informed my desire to write a book like this. But in those contexts, one's subject is *reading*, and one's task is to read interestingly, compellingly, to breathe new life for the current moment into works of literature, culture, detritus, what have you. There were, when I began this endeavor, the books of DeLillo I'd already read, sometimes multiply, and in varying states of excitement and memory over their contents. But when I write *academically* I am not solely writing from memory, and yet there does seem to be this desire to behave as though one is, to treat one's reading as a new detective treated their hours poring over images of decapitated torsos when one is faced in the real world with the genuine article. My own reading has never really been like this. My own reaction to DeLillo has run the gamut between excited laughter (*WN*, *GJS* in particular), awed sentence-worship (*RD, MII, PO, GJS, P, "BM", L*) and a real sense that there was a deep spiritual nature to writing, to working in language, and thus that I, in working to this scattered end, had *company*, had *guides* with pictures of their guides on their desks—DeLillo keeps, if memory serves, a picture of Borges where he works, that a friend gave him; and, perfectly enough, he admits to not knowing much or loving all of Borges, but simply liking the way the writer *looked*, and feeling compelled by something in the perceptible physical-writerly nature of the man. So in writing now, and quoting, and even in referring to these things I've read, and sometimes loved, and sometimes endured, but always did heed, what is it that you'd expect from such an exchange? Just what, precisely, are you hoping to get from this endeavor anyway?

◉ ◉ As the world of the image, first from newspapers and magazines, then films, then through advertising, billboards, television, personal computing, screens, and now smart phones, has rendered our world positively awash in imagery, no writer has remained so consistently preoccupied with this phenomenon as Writer has. What's doubly curious is Writer himself cited first *films* rather than other writing or writers that informed his work. What's interesting about this is Writer might be speaking about the perspective of not only *artists* in every medium at the time Godard's first films were releasing, but a great many human beings working in any industry at the time. The world was changing, and the ways of representing that world were explored in revelatory ways through Godard, or the slowed down films of Antonioni; so while fiction at the time was ouroborosing itself blue in the face, visual culture was exploding, violently, and Godard was a mere fragment of the ways in which what everything looked like, what people saw in a given day, was speeding up, exerting itself relentlessly so that even your average small town grocery store was suddenly awash in colors. And Writer was in New York City, where every second of every day there was something to see, something for the eye to get caught up in, some new fixation. So how do you write fiction speaking to the 70s, the 80s, the 90s, the 00s, the 2010s? If you're Writer, you *look* at these times. You look at positively everything. You watch the world transpiring. You digest it. You render it cleanly, the world within the world, and you continue to look, seeking in turn the word within the world. You continue to look, because by the time one book's out the thing has moved, and moved again between drafts. So you continue to look, and what happens? Over time, a body of work is amassed that is as minute yet widespread and far reaching as Dziga Vertov, a body of work that suddenly warps what fiction was, inverts the possibilities of novels, and short stories, and plays, and even journalism, and it does so because it's managed to let go of the strictures of literature and held onto instead the image, and the language in which the image is described. Again, per *Point Omega*: "It was only the closest watching that yielded this perception. He found himself undistracted for some minutes by the coming and going of others and he was able to look at the film with the degree of intensity that was required. The nature of the film permitted total concentration and also depended on it. The film's merciless pacing had no meaning without a corresponding watchfulness, the individual whose absolute alertness did not betray what was demanded. He stood and looked."

👁 👁 THE EYE IN *RUNNING DOG:* "You see them clustered, wrapped in whatever variety of coat or throwaway sweater or combination of these they've been able to acquire. […] "Eastward now, you see four letters spray-painted on the side of a building. Mongrel scrawl. ANGW. But familiar somehow, burning a hole in time. And it comes back now from a distance of more than twenty years. The visit to Salzburg. The cousins, the games, the museum. Four letters engraved on a ceremonial halberd. You father's explanation: *Alles nach Gottes Willen*. […] "Stacks of crates and cardboard boxes. A construction scaffold fronting an old building. Trucks and earth-moving equipment. Derelicts around a fire. Experience told him this is what he'd see. […] "…she was a discrepancy in the landscape. A welcome sight, sure, but also slightly disquieting—she didn't fit the picture. […] "He went to the front of the building and took a longer look at the scaffolding. He felt the dust in his eyes and mouth. Gannett watched from the front seat, sniffling a little. […] "The flashlight beam picked her out through clouds of plaster dust just as he was stepping through the window. He took a short-barreled .38 out of the shoulder holster under his lumber jacket and played the beam of light across the floor. He moved slowly forward, immediately wary of protruding nails, more generally concerned by the aura, the presences, a field of unnamed sensation. […] "Del Bravo looked for a weapon near the body. Plaster and wood dust filled his nostrils. He smelled perfume as well, and sweat, and noticed that her mascara had run and that the thick layer of face powder was cracked in places. No trace of pulse. The blood came out. He made his way back to the window. […] "Probably the single biggest difference between old and new styles of erotic art is the motion picture. The movie. The image that moves. This assumes you consider movies art.' [..] "The last light went out and Moll stood in shadow in the open doorway, unable to see Lightborne at all. […] "The temperature kept dropping but this didn't signify change. It signified intensity. It signified a concentration of the faculty of recall. A steadiness of image. No stray light.

It was snowing in the mountains.

[…] "He was twenty yards from the barracks when he realized two cats were at his feet. He stopped and turned. Three more cats moved this way. He knew what it meant. Still more cats came out from under the barracks. They followed him, moving around his feet, mewing. Cats approached from another direction now, the windmill. An image unwinding. After ten paces he crouched down and they were all over and around him, scratching, crying out, at least fifteen cats and kittens, allowing themselves to be petted and rubbed, or just stretching in the sun, purring, or sniffing at his clothes, all of them looking healthy and well fed."

RD, 1, 3, 4, 5, 6, 18, 22, 192, 223

👁 👁 Is the flashlight's beam an acceptable surrogate for the eye? I find myself thinking. I find myself up against the limitations of writing anything meaningful, but then too against the temptation of saying something that truly has not been said about any artist. Really, anybody at all. I hope to write new things. Writer writes new things. Writer's books, each one of them, for any flaws that surely exist, feel genuinely novel, feel genuinely new. This is the ambition, which means the flashlight poring over the body in *Running Dog* counts, attached as it is to the man, Del Bravo, and it's here I can imagine someone arguing he's psyching himself up for the big pushes of *Underworld*, but there's something warmer here, less perfected and cold, a flashlight held in a meaty hand in a building largely abandoned, making sense of the world in the detective's way—slowly, slowly—and the language around it could be the language of Elmore Leonard, sure, but it's just slightly more exactingly clipped, and the thought that this too could be contained within the critical project is what compels me, small as it may be—*Running Dog,* rated basically not at all by any recognizable machine, though referenced for the Hitler curiosity, feels like the Writer in any documentary, so the eyes are the paranoid kind, and the language is a paranoiac's misremembering of the comforts of Ed McBain, so there is the fleshy warmth of the ambling city presence, the body, the man, the holding of the flashlight, and it hasn't quite been shorn of its imperfections yet, which in turn will have its purpose. It embodies the stilling of the world in both Gordon's *24 Hour Psycho* and *Point Omega*, the honing of attention to its point, through its preoccupation with light and shadow, with film, with observing and finally with attention, with reading, since we're moving through the strangeness of the novel just the same as its figures, as Writer himself, word by word illuminating the world. "The temperature kept dropping but this didn't signify change. It signified intensity. It signified a concentration of the faculty of recall. A steadiness of image. No stray light. It was snowing in the mountains."

👁 👁 We now exist within a culture obsessed by the image, which is to say we live in a culture obsessed with that with which it can distract itself, which does not mean the image is easy, a "dumber" way to spend one's time. In fact it's probably putting it too dramatically to say that it's a culture obsessed only with that with which it can distract itself. That is an effect. The image, though, comes first. The image is not simply easy. The image, too, is not dumber. It isn't even really worth considering these things in these terms. The image simply is, and we are simply fixated, and that is our culture. In the 1950s, American literature seemed largely concerned with reckoning with World War II, and quickly shifted to being concerned with Experience, by way of Kerouac's *On the Road*, and a certain absurdity as articulated by William Burroughs in *Naked Lunch*, and certain precedent texts. This wasn't uniform, considering still the sales of *Peyton Place* and the works of James Jones, contemporaneously, anyway, but we are now concerned with the dregs. Looking back, what we get are the dregs. The dregs hold Kerouac and they hold Burroughs. First, a yearning: Experience, Go West, do something more than join Uncle Sam's army. Then, an absurdity: Move to Greenwich Village, get stoned on Tea, consider Breton, Picasso, see avant garde films, embrace disruption. The concerns of the Americans were simultaneously large and small, local and global, but largely the work for Kerouac seemed still reflective of the strain of realism established way back when Flaubert wrote his early works. Burroughs represented a departure, also informed by the image, though in his case the images of concern were abstract paintings, which Burroughs and Brion Gysin viewed as markedly "ahead" of literature, warranting a strain of experimentation previously unprecedented in writing. The guiding light, at least in the prompting of the creation of this strain, did seem to be these images, these painted works. It was not about depicting the world how it was, for them. It was about advancing the form to advance the world. It was about newness, but not merely newness at face value, i.e. grabbing at whatever might present itself that didn't register as literature, as writing. It was about finding something, for Burroughs and Co. the pursuit of art, of intoxication, of Scientology, of dreaming experiments. For Kerouac, some of these, and drink, and Buddhism, and traveling, movement, and frenetic writing by way of caffeine and amphetamines. For Writer, it begins with some reading, Faulkner, Hemingway, etc., pursuit of career in advertising, quit of advertising career, saving money and going to the movies, observing the world.

👁 👁 In the 1960s the notable shift in American literature, just before Writer begins to cut his teeth, is inward, orbital, centripetal, embracing a self-referentiality that really hasn't finished being exhausted. Writers as diverse as Robert Coover, Joan Didion, Truman Capote, James Baldwin, and Tom Wolfe begin to use their direct experience to generate compelling material, processing—through the eye—reality in prose that's sometimes exhaustive and sprawling, minimalist and acute, spreading and obsessive and ruminative, declarative and intuitive and spiritual, or as bright and plasticky as a walk down the aisle at any contemporaneous supermarket. The image and the eye matter because subjectivity matters, i.e. *it all matters, and herein I intend to prove it.* There are moments of great reinvention, too, for the Novel as an entity, especially within America, that Writer inherits, and that influence and inform his sense of—and really any following writer's sense of—the potential space he'll occupy, the moment in the public consciousness. Writers like Norman Mailer, particularly, bringing together the crashing forces of his ridiculous personal existence and the Pentagon-levitating impulses of present history evoke a kind of mystical, shamanistic vein for the fiction writer that Kesey, still Burroughs, Didion certainly, Coover certainly, Pynchon certainly each too seem invested in chipping away at. It is also the era wherein Writer is truly coming of age. The era of America's long and ridiculous conflict in Vietnam. The era of the death of John Fitzgerald Kennedy by assassination. The beginning of the myths of Nixon, the developing CIA and FBI, and all of it being projected directly into the home, into storefront windows, into everyday average American experience like never before, on TV.

👁 👁 What's notable too in the movement from the 1960s onward is there seems to be the dawning of a real antipathy towards the perceived reading public and American writers of a certain kind. John Barth, Thomas Pynchon, and others later lumped into the "postmodern" school (a term now about as useless as a term could be, via J. Peterson et al) began making work that seemed to aspire to contain all the world, chockfull of fireworks and experimentation, a potential read on the whole matter being *I don't give a shit if you read this, they'll read it in Paris—I am an artist, the public are dipshits—I don't write for them.* This is OK, and an important turn in every culture, but one only need look at examples of it still being written in the year 2025 to understand how limited and limiting it proves as a view of the Novel. Although exceptions existed in every preceding era—just a quick glance at *The Autobiography of Alice B. Toklas*, *The Sun Also Rises*, and *The Sound and the Fury* are sufficient to highlight it's inept to consider any uniformity in pre-1950s work in the Novel that Writer's inheriting—the notion of different schools of thought in the Novel, within the same country, with vastly differing inclinations, concerns, and subject matter feels new. For all the experimentation of these or the aforementioned, there are still incredibly conventional novels being published and being bestsellers, family sagas and multigenerational pastoral works that offer pockets into which any writer might find themselves if they read X first and fall in love compared with Y. The city, of course, is a factor. New York City in particular. And New York City in the late 1960s and early 1970s is an incredibly polarized entity, especially considering it in terms of the eye, the image. Writer's childhood in the Bronx is often spoken of almost idyllically, with scenes of stickball and sitting at the apartment window listening to radio broadcasts of baseball games. There was certainly disorder, and poverty, but the rift into the '60s and especially into the '70s begins to grow like the maw of an awful beast. Scenes of squalor next to affluence to an impossible degree. New money colliding with old and spitting out its refuse into the Lower East Side. Filth scattered on the streets commingled with moments of great patriotic verve—often tied to sport, though the media itself is growing and the throb and flicker of places like Times Square begin reverberating out throughout Manhattan and the outer boroughs now, the eye drawn to endless coiling neon tubes and TV sets, the Moon Landing and the voice of Walter Cronkite orating tribally as one world gives way to another. Lee Harvey Oswald lives nearby him in his youth.

This realization informing the intimacy of *Libra*, and too of Writer's growing preoccupation post-1970s with violence, with terrorism, as just as emblematic of the spectacle of American life as any of these markers. DeLillo's beginning context, then, is busy, and crowded, and charged with a sense of invention; both for the Novel and for American life more generally. *Americana*, then, is the apparatus through which Writer first articulates his place in the world *as* a writer, and it reads unlike most any first novel that I can think of, in part because of its prodigious focus on the image and its relationship to Writer's generation of Americans, and probably more exactly American writers and artists.

◉ ◉ THE EYE IN *AMERICANA*: "My own instincts led me to Kirk Douglas and Burt Lancaster. These were the American pyramids and they needed no underground to spread their fame. They were monumental. Their faces slashed across the screen. When they laughed or cried it was without restraint. Their chromium smiles were never ambiguous. And they rarely had time to sit down and trade cynical quips with some classy society dame or dumb flatfoot. They were men of action, running, leaping, loving with abandon. When I was a teenager I saw Burt in *From Here to Eternity*. He stood above Deborah Kerr on that Hawaiian beach and for the first time in my life I felt the true power of the image. Burt was like a city in which we are all living. He was that big. Within the conflux of shadow and time, there was room for all of us and I knew I must extend myself until the molecules parted and I was spliced into the image. Burt in the moonlight was a crescendo of male perfection but no less human because of it. Burt lives! I carry that image to this day, and so, I believe, do millions of others, men and women, for their separate reasons. Burt in the moonlight. It was a concept; it was the icon of a new religion."

A, 12

 [8]

[8] Cropped screenshot of Burt Lancaster and Deborah Kerr from the film *From Here to Eternity* (1953).

👁 👁 I'm both old and young enough to remember a time when this kind of image-worship was possible, and to feel a sense of yearning for it now that image distribution has become so exquisitely speedy and abundant that stable entities like Hollywood stars don't hold nearly the weight they once did. They only do if they're co-opted into these disparate contexts and can become commingled into meme language and repurposed as modes of interpersonal communication. Worship didn't quite seem like the perfect word for it, image-worship, but at the same time the religious practice of worship often involves a *lack* of conscious action, or a willing towards a lack of conscious action, which strikes me as pretty much the exact same thing as both how we once stared up at film screens and how we now stare into smartphones. I like viewing the characterization of Burt Lancaster as "a city in which we were all living" as a new, unexpected iteration of McLuhan's "Global village". Unexpected because most discussions of interconnected media technologies still frequently (but not exclusively, to be fair) concern themselves with the user as a locus of communication. They certainly are, but what's weird are the ways in which these central figures, conveyed in images, worshiped as images, organize these interconnected media technologies, frequently affecting the ways in which they develop—I'm thinking of various booms, often involving moneymaking, on places like Instagram, Twitter/X, Patreon, and elsewhere, often brought about either by celebrities who enter these environments with an image actively being worshiped, or by mircocelebrities who've slowly built themselves up as images to be worshiped so they're able to monetize said image. I can almost feel myself yearning, when reading this, for a time when the world could stably get behind a Burt Lancaster, not simply as a character in a film but as an "American pyramid," as something offering a shape and context to our existence in the world, calibrating our sufferings and our sense of our mortality and our romantic existence in a relatively uniform manner. Each generation seems beholden to the kinds of images it worships. The more singular the images—i.e., Stalin, Jesus, FDR—the easier it seems to be to unify huge swaths of a population toward particular ends. There will always be discrepancies, but when the world offered fewer, and stabler images to worship, there seemed to be more and potentially more interesting things the populace might do with them—think, e.g., of the abundant and far-reaching theories around a certainly stable, and relatively simple image like the U.S. dollar bill, an icon so frequently paranoically analyzed the practice of doing so has been satirized many times over. It is perhaps indicative of Writer's growing sense of the image and of modern life that as images and their worship have grown more abundant, his late works have grown cleaner, shorter, more overtly textual, and if they are concerned with images, it's often in the manner of *Point Omega*, where one thing is reflected on intently and intensely, as opposed to *Americana*, where though we have moments like this reflection on Burt Lancaster, fifty feet high on screen, we have far more moments that seem to anticipate the world in 2025, staring through personal cameras at any and everything, observing life relentlessly and with as much speed and intensity as it can offer us. The scales of image-worship somehow got flipped. The desiring engine of that 1970s America, that littered its storefronts with TVs, got miniaturized and inverted; one screen, or maybe two, with a relentless feed the multiple TV sets once provided over the course of a week transmitted in mere seconds.

👁 👁 I am not interested in asking questions about the specific experience of reading a single text. This is not what I mean in referring to this work as a work interested in reading itself. What I mean in saying this is that even the aspects of this text that fall into that chasm bore me terribly, and all that I'm able to do for them is apologize, because I know there will be more of them, and this troubles me. I am interested in the experience of reading an author, and Writer, Don DeLillo in particular, and in carrying such an experience with you. And perhaps, too, instead of approaching this work in the manner of say Nicholson Baker, in his wondrous *U & I*, a book that has influenced me more than almost any other, I won't limit myself to not reading any further sentences from Writer's work, but I'll try and limit myself to this perspective on his work, perspective, really, being the operative word, concerned as I am with the eye. I dislike the scholarly convention, though, of proving points. Again, I hate the ways in which this text has already fallen victim to such an impulse. In some ways, I am a coward and a failure, and again, all that I can do is apologize. What I mean in saying all of this is that I am curious about the relationship I *now* have, right now, with an author's work. With the reading of their work, and with re-engagement with it, in my mind, yes, and also via text, via quoted sections, via the conceit or overall constructed element of the eye and a mode of reading Writer's work. When I reflect on the experience of watching a film, for instance, I can find myself *driven*. I can find myself *compelled*. I can replay things that were said and I can feel *better* about my life. What equivalencies to this exist for the act of reading? What do we carry with us, effectively, from an author's work? What do I, now, carry with me from Writer's work? A novel is not a story that starts and ends. This from Writer is a kind of truism. A novel is not a story that starts and ends. A novel is not even a text of 50,000 or more words. *The Silence* is a novel, and probably reaches 13,000 words, if that. *The Silence* is an American novel, by Writer, about things, perhaps, but I don't think that's my relationship to it. A novel being "about" things, per Writer, is one of the least interesting qualities of a novel. Probably one text in Writer's oeuvre refutes this, being *Libra*. *Libra* is "about" something. However, if you told someone what *Libra* was about, and asked them, based on this, to reconstruct it—well, you can see, probably whether you've read *Libra* or not, knowing only that it's a text about Lee Harvey Oswald, written by Writer, that it's hopelessly ridiculous.

👁 👁 I saw a Pollock painting in person for the first time at the Art Institute in Chicago. I don't necessarily believe that it is necessary to view all artworks in person, if we feel an artwork we *haven't* seen in person is meaningful to us. I will say, in this case, because of my relationship with both the work of Pollock, and with the man himself, seeing his work in person felt eventually necessary. When seeing it, I stood, and I stared, not unlike a character in Writer's work. Thinking about this, I struggle to think of meaningful reading experiences wherein a figure stands and looks at an artwork they perceive as meaningful. What's more, per the critics, per Hickey and Ruskin and Hazlitt, it's curious that I don't remember as many moments in their works wherein they stand and look at something in that context. The work is treated as a given, perhaps. Writer, and Dostoevsky, in *The Idiot*, with "The Body of the Dead Christ in the Tomb," the painting by Hans Holbein the Younger—and, incidentally, the painting that affected Dostoevsky so viscerally he stood, day after day, not unlike a character in Writer, staring at it while traveling, ignoring all else. It seems curious that this experience finds itself best realized in novels, in fictional contexts, rather than in the work of the critics. I saw Magritte's "The Banquet" and wrote about it for an art history class I took. I didn't know who'd painted it, as I'd approached it, but something about it drew me in. If you've seen it, you know what I mean. If you haven't seen it, there's a large bright red dot in the center of an otherwise pretty conventional image of a balcony looking out over a forest. It is a magnetic thing. Again, I stared at it for a long time. I had read *Mao II*, prior to this. I was gearing up to see the Mao painting the Art Institute had. It was upstairs, so first I went to these other rooms and experienced these other works. I felt myself welling up with something. Not with tears, really, but a kind of energy. The energy, though, was informed by my reading of Writer. The energy was connected with these stories of these people in rooms looking at things. The Warhol was on the top floor, in this wing that abutted the varied sculptures and gardens in the park where Lollapalooza takes over each summer. I didn't have any idea what to expect. I'd never been a massive fan of Warhol, as I'd really only known him through paintings people did recreating his Marilyn Monroe images in high school classes. Later, I'd come to really love his work, his writing in particular, and a photograph Richard Avedon took of Warhol after he was shot by Valerie Solanas—itself a perfectly Writerly thing—remains one of my favorite images ever; but at the time my expectations weren't too high. I had, however, been awed by Writer's novel, and by a more ambient sense of the artwork, which was reprinted on the cover, but wasn't treated in the same way "24 Hour Psycho" is treated in *Point Omega*, e.g., or the "Baader-Meinhof" paintings of Gerhard Richter were treated in that short story—I thought this, at the time, and I'm writing this now in the interest of full disclosure, but in the interest of full disclosure I feel an anxiety that perhaps there *are* scenes in *Mao II* wherein the paintings are looked at precisely in this way, but noting the weird experience of reading something after you've finished with the book—it does seem true, as Tan Lin indicated somewhere, that we read something far longer than when we simply sit down and read it, we continue reading something, and per the thing I recall but can't find at present because it may or may not be real (itself another facet of all of this; it may be in a video, or on one of the few podcasts he's been interviewed on)—I'll keep these things because they are true to my experience as a kind of test subject in this work in considering reading Writer's texts. I'd walked into the room so that the wall the painting was on was behind me and to my right. I entered, via pathways through other galleries, containing other artworks, around an open corner, which was closed off facing the Warhol painting, but leaving the painting and the room it was contained in wide open. I hadn't followed a map or anything, just seen it indicated where the painting would approximately be, so I went there. I remember I turned around and the size of the image was perfectly astounding, entirely stupefying. I really couldn't believe it, seemingly could not take it in. Mao's image, with assorted colors, had taken up a wall that might've been as high as twenty or thirty feet, it seemed. The image was just so massive. It was later in the day, and I was alone in the room, and so I sat down on the ground against the wall which held a door to leave that part of the gallery behind me. I sat down, and stared up, and felt myself awed by this experience. I probably knew little, very little, of Mao himself. I don't think I really knew much of anything of Warhol either, and didn't care to know. I knew of this one work, however, in the context of having finished the novel, and the experience, like the eating of various things during the reading of various things, completely overwhelmed me, and seemed to saturate me, and seemed to enrich me as I considered the feeling of reading the text, on the floor, there, in the gallery, looking up, of the experience of sitting on the train, and seeing the notice that the paintings were coming to Chicago, and felt myself centered, and breathed out a massive amount of air, flattening my stomach and shrinking my diaphragm, and looked with new eyes upon the world.

👁 👁 Nicholas Branch, and the CIA, and the Zapruder film. One of perhaps five of the most significant events in America in a decade lousy with them. Perhaps one of the ten most significant events in a country's history, rendered on a handheld camera, by a man in Dallas, Texas. We don't just have the film, reimagined fictively, as a "scene" in a novel, we have the person observing the thing, in an official capacity. In the following paragraphs it's categorized, like so much other government detritus. We have a man, and a mission, and the mission is to observe, to look, to watch this thing and try to make sense of it. Because suddenly, whether it's JFK's assassination, or it's a monk burning alive, or it's a group of men pointing from a balcony towards an assassin, suddenly *these* are the things that people our world; the images, the videos, the *representations* of existence, through which we're able to make sense of things. They, too, are our pyramids, our Burt Lancasters, of a unique and paranoiac darkness. A cursory glance at "Zapruder film" even on Amazon presents a wide range of opportunities through which it can be engaged. So DeLillo isn't alone in his preoccupation with the looked-at as the thing to devote one's energy to in writing. He's well ahead of the curve in this respect, but decade after decade since *Americana* came out his devotion to what he sees has put him in an entirely different world as a novelist. He's carved out new paths not just for literature but for culture more broadly speaking, as every corner of contemporary life is filled with watching, with watching others watching, with watching disturbing things, conspiracy-driven things, esoteric things, forbidden things. Somehow, in a career that really hasn't seen much in the way of repetition—thematically, sure, but every book is markedly distinct—he's articulated an impassioned testimony to written art, and a way forward for anyone bemoaning the declining of reading versus the ascendancy of visual culture.

PHOTOGRAPH FROM ZAPRUDER FILM

PHOTOGRAPH THROUGH RIFLE SCOPE [9]

9 Z222 from Zapruder film plus view from sniper's nest taken from reenactment, CE888-2, https://commons.wikimedia.org/wiki/File:Z222_from_Zapruder_film_plus_view_from_sniper%27s_nest_taken_from_reenactment,_CE888-2.jpg

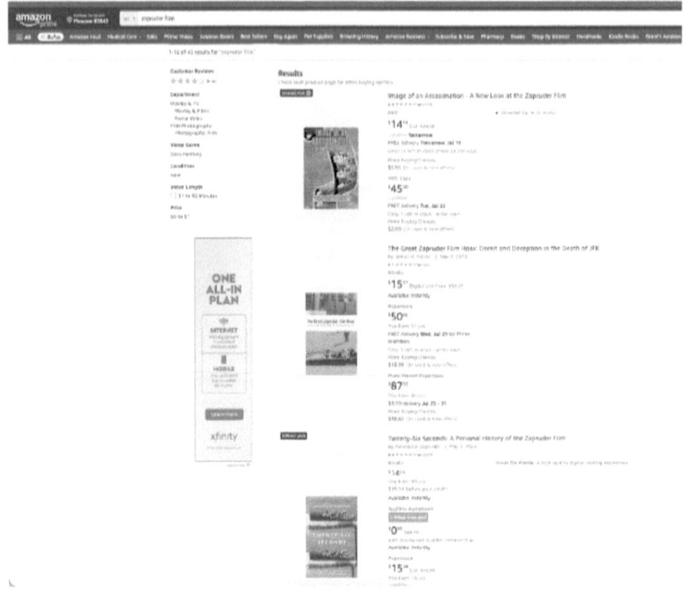

[10]

[11]

[10] Amazon search results for "Zapruder Film" screenshot.

[11] YouTube search results for "Zapruder Film" screenshot.

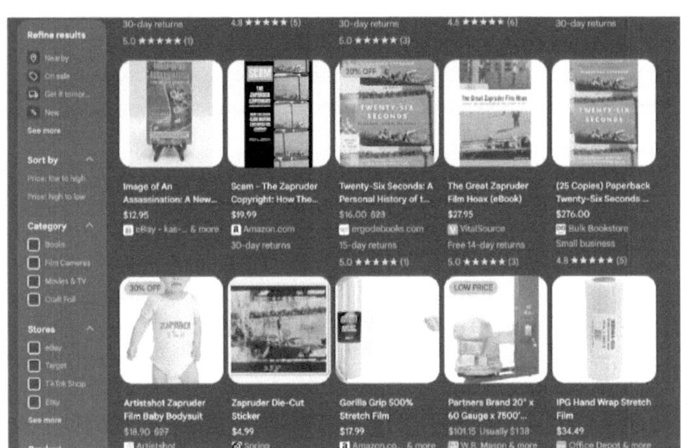

12

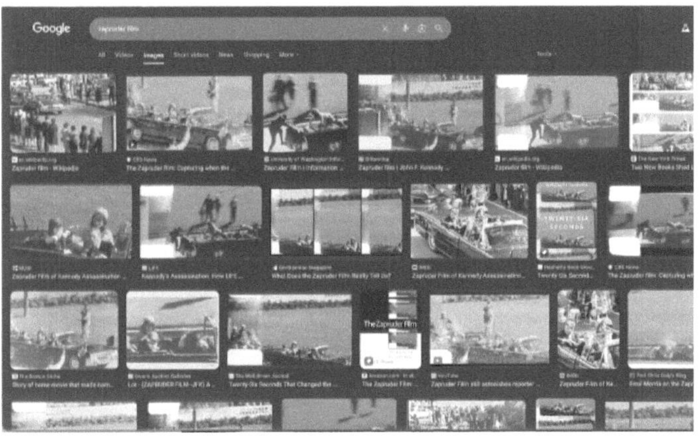

13

[12] Google Shopping search results for “zapruder film” screenshot.

[13] Google Images search results for “zapruder film” screenshot.

👁 👁 THE EYE OF NICHOLAS BRANCH IN *LIBRA*: "The stuff keeps coming. The Curator sends FBI surveillance logs. He sends a thirty-five-hour film chronology of unedited network footage shot during the weekend of November 22. He sends a computer-enhanced version of the Zapruder film, the 8mm home movie made by a dress manufacturer who stood on a concrete abutment above Elm Street as the shots were fired. Experts have scrutinized every murky nuance of the Zapruder film. It is the basic timing device of the assassination and a major emblem of uncertainty and chaos. There is the powerful moment of death, the surrounding blurs, patches and shadows.

(Branch's analysis of the film and other evidence leads him to believe the first shot came much sooner than most theories would allow, probably at Zapruder frame 186. Governor Connally was hit two point six seconds later, at Zapruder 234. The shot that killed the President, crushingly, came four point three seconds after that. Even though he has reached firm conclusions in this area, Branch will study the computerized version of Zapruder. He is in too deep to stop now.)"

L, 441

👁 👁 He is also, here, depicting the impulse driving not only those who become fixated on JFK's assassination, but those who become fixated on almost any image, any picture, especially those that move. The only way out for Branch is through. The only way out for anyone is through. Because of its speed, the assassination of JFK really is the first national tragedy of its kind in America, and it's significant both for this and because it's something that's continued to happen again and again. While not exactly the same in terms of the killing's direct result, i.e. the death of an American president, it's something that in its indirect effects on the populace has been reiterated, initially every decade or so, but now happening easily every calendar year, sometimes more frequently than this. Any event since JFK's assassination that's had people glued to TV sets, smartphones, newsfeeds of any kind, is something equivalent in its tragedy, give or take, to the populace. It is shocking, incomprehensible, and spreads itself out in a weird, talky, cancerous manner of paranoiac thinking that contributes to mountains of text, lifetimes of devotion to speculation and efforts to understand, and less and less trust that things are precisely what they seem. It makes sense, then, that Writer looks back to it when he's doing a sort of lifework, an endeavor to hang his hat on, as it were, to articulate something definitive about what his perception of art really is. The book sort of pulls us through the Warren Commission Report Lite, which makes sense considering Writer read all of it in preparation, but it's in the Branch sections I tend to feel most at home, most like I'm witnessing something near and dear to Writer's heart, a preoccupation that runs through most of what he's written, this fixation on looking, on watching. "The shot that killed the President, crushingly, came four point three seconds after that. Even though he has reached firm conclusions in this area, Branch will study the computerized version of Zapruder. He is in too deep to stop now.)" One can't escape the feeling that this now applies to all of us, with easy access to an impossible amount of horrific and in-depth material about every single thing. Though our method often diverges completely from Branch's monastic focus, there's something warming in this sense that the watcher can have a unique utility in the modern world, the person not only able to discern particulars with shrewdness, but who seems best utilized in that context for mankind.

👁 👁 THE EYE IN GUY DEBORD: "The images detached from every aspect of life fuse in a common stream in which the unity of this life can no longer be reestablished. Reality considered partially unfolds, in its own general unity, as a pseudo-world apart, an object of mere contemplation. The specialization of images of the world is completed in the world of the autonomous image, where the liar has lied to himself. The spectacle in general, as the concrete inversion of life, is the autonomous movement of the non-living."

👁 👁 If the literature of Writer could be said to have heroes—it does, of course, though it's not the kind of thing one might naturally think of when thinking of Writer's work; he tends, in my estimation, to be the kind of writer people come to view as the hero of his work, which isn't a problem but a fact, or at least partially factual—then Nicholas Branch is one, and his struggle is an heroic one, and his determination to persist in what he's doing is an heroic one. It is because of the characterization of Debord, or rather because of the net messaging of Debord's characterization, that Branch can be viewed as an heroic figure. What I take from the image in Debord is the sense that we now have of the image, and in particular the spectacular image, is winning, so to speak, in the war for human consciousness. Nowadays it almost seems patently obvious, blatant. There's a sense that we are overwhelmed, which is obvious, but overwhelmed with a kind of intent, not necessarily established by a singular cadre of manipulators, though certainly they've got their hands in the pot as well, but by the sheer power of the spectacle and the spectacular image itself. There is, of course, the concrete economic/political lineage Debord is drawing from, as there is the logical/philosophical tradition Wittgenstein is drawing from, and in either circumstance I only really have continuing interest in the offspring of those lineages, those traditions, in Debord and Wittgenstein, so I've got to sort of shrug, and take what I can get, and hope I'm not making any bigger a mess than I'm making in reading anything the way I've read it, but there seems to be an attempt to push back against this overwhelming tide, and I think it's possible to view the efforts of a writer like Writer as largely enacting this, as trying to undo manipulation, especially manipulation via language—again, recalling, he got his start in advertising—by offering us, instead of poetry, instead of mere fiction for its own sake, for the sake of "story," or "entertainment," or any of the linchpins often invoked as the fundamental motivators for reading either fiction or poetry; with Writer we get something between these poles, and often even between the third outer gravity of nonfiction, as Writer frequently—as in *Libra*, of course—draws directly on actual existence, actual historical evidence and truth, to give us something speaking to an alternative current of language for our world. This, Writer's career seems to assert, is the only thing a writer ought to become preoccupied with in the long term.

👁 👁 THE EYE IN WRITER: "Let's say that European and Asian cinemas of the 1960s shaped the way I think and feel about things. At that time I was living in New York, I didn't have much money, didn't have much work, I was living in one room … I was a man in a small room. And I went to the movies a lot, watching Bergman, Antonioni, Godard. When I was little, in the Bronx, I didn't go to the cinema and I didn't think of the American films I saw as works of art. Perhaps, in an indirect way, cinema allowed me to become a writer. In *Americana*, my first novel, the main character ends his journey with a camera on his shoulder, making home movies. There's a phrase in a Godard movie that refers to the young people of 1968, "the children of Marx and Coca-Cola." In *Americana* a character refers to the "children of Godard and Coca-Cola."[14]

[14] "A Conversation with Don DeLillo: Has Terrorism Become the World's Main Plot?" *Panic* #1, Nov. 2005, pp. 90-95.

👁 👁 I don't know what a contemporary *Americana* or Godard would refer to this generation, now, in 2025, as. Coca Cola seems largely to have gone out in popularity. We are now the children of Red Bull or Celsius and LiveLeak, or Jehu to follow Godard's construction. This is the element that, more than anything else, compelled me in this direction, because in reading Writer I don't know that I ever felt myself tapping into any novelistic tradition. I didn't grow up particularly caring about novels or novelists. I cared about TV, and I cared about movies, and in time I wanted to read and to write, but only late, and only in particular ways, drawn to particular things rather than the whole of it all. I can't speak to whether Writer was precisely the same, but this idea from this interview does seem to convey at least some sense of not being wholly influenced as a novelist/Writer by other novelists/writers exclusively. To many, this is an obvious thing. In other artforms, this is a more obvious thing. Songwriters talk about poets, and other writers, in other forms, who've influenced them, or films. Sculptors draw on the real world and the fictional world, the verifiable "true" world and the world of an imagination, or the world of others' imaginations, creating works that blur the lines between these spaces, alien creatures or large abstract structures like Jeff Koons', that refer to objects in reality but cranked up really high and absurd, commercial and a little dumb. With writers, there tends to be this sense, often conveyed by professors who haven't managed to succeed fully as writers, that to officially become a member of the professional authorial class you have to be embedded deeply in your tradition, you have to have done precisely the reading they want you to do, and you have to want to do more. Of course, Writer did his reading, and remains interested in the work that writers are continuing to do, and remains invested in his sense of what literature can be. But the standout element in his work is its tendency to elude that stable tradition, creating books that operate on an internal logic that's made out of this perfect mixture of Writer's consciousness and the real world as observed by Writer's consciousness. This statement, or this idea, that a writer can be made from a love of film, rather than a love first and foremost of books, or a love first and foremost of writing itself, seems endlessly important for a generation existing more in the throes of the question of reading's place in the world than any preceding it. If the kind of writing Writer does is to survive at all, really, it seems imperative that writers learn to embrace new paths to the waterfall, as it were, to crib a phrase from Raymond Carver.

👁 👁 THE NOVEL IN *SEVEN CONTROLLED VOCABULARIES AND OBITUARY 2004, the JOY OF COOKING* BY TAN LIN: "The ideal novel would not be necessary to read at all. It would have no inside or outside. All words would flow outwards like soft data. All "events" would be migratory or reduced to background clutter. All novels would aspire to the condition of Muzak. Production, dissemination and consumption would become one. All attention would be leftover for an indeterminate amount of time. No one would fall asleep while reading a book again. Aristotle was wrong. A novel like an event should not take place in 24 hours or less. Comprehension would cease to matter or would be deflected so that all actions would seem to be taking place "somewhere else." Or not at all. Or in slow motion. Or invisibly. Or against the grain of the visible. As everyone who has ever watched a TV show about nature or wild animals mating can tell you, beauty like reading lies in increasing forms of inexactitude. It is best to behave like an animal or an insect when reading. In this way reading is more readily absorbed by the human body. The most beautiful things in a novel are the things one didn't know one was thinking about. For this reason, a novel should not tell a story of anything in particular. It should be an exercise in non-attention and non-development and the gradual erasure of content. Of course all of this inexactitude, non-comprehension and nonmemory should all take place in time and be subject to duration rather than chronology. Smaller fonts are more readily absorbed by the eye. I have never felt like an insect except when I was in high school and I was asked to make a miniature pencil holder in shop class."

👁 👁 Lin's book, sometimes shortened to *7CV*, is technically poetry, but if this excerpt is any indication to those unfamiliar with Lin's work, it eludes easy categorization, often embracing sampling, weird experiments with software, and other means of disrupting the traditional function and apparatus of the book, the writer, and certainly the poet. He's one of the only theorists of reading I have any interest in, and when I say reading I mean reading and writing. He seems to be one of the only writers actually engaging the world as it presently exists, though I'd also include Writer in this, and yet because Writer developed his method and was acknowledged for the success of this method in the twentieth century, there can be some feeling of his work being perfectly apt to eight to ten years ago—this isn't intended as an insult, when the vast majority of writers still write as if we were the same readers that existed in 1950, or worse, 1880. When I think of reading now I think of this "non-attention and non-development and the gradual erasure of content," the moments of long drift wherein I've had pages open in front of me, or on a screen, or in the corner of a screen cluttered with material, data, digital effluvia, wherein I'm inconsistently able to retain, to hold fast to an image, a scene playing out in my head, or the wonderment of language, split into lines before me, trying and succeeding to make sense of it. Then there are these long stretches wherein I feel myself retaining nothing, but I am in fact reading, and I can in fact recall aspects of what I'm reading, and I am experiencing something that I can register as meaningful, if not personally, then at least aesthetically—I'm able to do something with it. I think, again, of John Cage's *Writing Through Finnegans Wake*, of engaging with a book of necessity in a new way, because we want to read it, and we want to engage with it, and we want to have done both, and yet, in part because of "the concrete inversion of life, is the autonomous movement of the non-living" (Debord), i.e. the spectacle, these whirring forces brittling our consciousnesses and blunting our simple living, we must adjust. I don't mean to so negatively characterize it, because I don't wish to treat it, per se. I wish to treat the matters I deeply value, like Writer, and Lin, and reading and writing and art and the making and consumption of these things. The work that Writer does—again, I am weirdly partial to the late period books, because he seems to be enacting, in a way, what Lin is advocating, in a way—feels cognizant of these historical realities, as opposed to insisting upon the undeniable necessity of his work, seems to wish to push the work into places that give it a sense of its necessity, derived not from the contexts of genre, nor even larger genre categories like Novel, Short Story, whatever, articulating only its necessity as language.

◉ ◉ THE EYE RETURNS IN *AMERICANA*: "I hurried toward the hotel, my pockets full of scraps of paper, index cards, neatly creased sheets, Scotch-taped fragments, throwaways uncrumpled and hand-pressed, what detritus and joy, a grainy day, child of Godard and Coca-Cola.

I asked the desk clerk, an old man this time whose face was purplish with broken blood vessels, if he could turn up a portable TV set somewhere in the building. I needed it for an hour and I was willing to slip a discreetly folded five-dollar bill into the breast pocket of his sturdy mail-order shirt. He came up later carrying the thing, a bulky Motorola, as if it were a wounded man he could not wait to deposit somewhere. I plugged it in, turned the sound down to nothing, then set the Canon Scoopic on the tripod."

A, 269

👁 👁 *Americana* almost certainly is not the first novel written to prominently feature home video cameras. It is, however, the first to use them so intently as a device capable of rounding out a character's world. What's interesting, too, is that much of the speculative fiction published for the hundred or so years prior to *Americana*'s existence doesn't anticipate the personification, the sort of osmotic relationship people will come to have with their technology. Mostly these are moral tales, with new technology, and at most they provide cautionary suggestion as to where this sort of rampant industrialization and consumerism and militarism might lead humanity. In terms of the daily shifts, however, either in literature or in film, the technology is always something happening in an otherwise stable, historical/contemporaneous world. This is largely true because for human being it was largely true. The advent of the television didn't exactly change matters, along these lines. The television set was a more streamlined iteration of the radio, and the radio a more streamlined version of weekly entertainments at the theater, perhaps the movies. Things didn't seem to really change considerably until the user gained an ability to communicate back with their technology. First, the telephone, which altered things slightly, but the lack of expectation that these were going to be recorded things limited its reach. For years, a still camera was too expensive for most of the people of the world to own. A person might live all their life with only five or ten photographs taken of them well into the 1960s, and then the costs began to shift. Suddenly photographs were ways of commenting on one's reality, one's existence. Suddenly art photography begins to change, get more personal, more subjective, communicating things both prior painting and prior photography couldn't necessarily access. It's a stretch, certainly, but perhaps not totally outside the realm of possibility that the harrowing photographs of Vietnam were increased in their efficacy because of that moment's camera ubiquity. No longer were war photographs these packaged things, made with instruments most of humanity would never touch, let alone own, and would only encounter in very extenuating circumstances, and thus the photographs themselves were slightly at a remove from one's existence. With Vietnam, a similar camera to the one many people might have on their shelf took the photographs of children in Vietnam with their clothing burned. War was no longer this completely elusive thing. All of it was now connected. In *Americana*, both its protagonist David Bell's career, working largely in televisual advertising, and his practice of making films, of recording his existence, of responding to situations by getting out his film camera and making sense of his world that way, reflect at once a shift happening then in America, toward the recording of one's life as a means of making it matter, of making meaning, and towards the sense that these new modes of technology were somehow changing the landscape beyond media, extending now to experience, such that the probably useless items in Bell's pockets are listed much in the way Lester Bangs might set the scene of a wild show at CBGB's. The weird polarity between what used to be the world of celebrity where any detail matters, we'll take all of it, has begun moving towards this new reality we're presently experiencing where some random person, a Nobody, can jump to the fore in everyone's consciousness, have their life matter, the detail matter in a way historically only reserved for those already deemed exceptional. It also represents a throughline in Writer's work, from Bell, to Branch, to the protagonists in both "Baader-Meinhof" and *Point Omega*—these people fixated on fixation, on observing, on a kind of visual data processing that, in our present, could not be more vital. Writer seems to be saying, more or less, that this is an essential thing both of the present, the 1970s, 80s, and onward, and the future; the ability to record, to pay close attention and to discern, to curate one's existence amid this technology, to make one's sense of it. In some ways it extends too to Bill Gray's weird moments of blowing and cleaning the hairs from his typewriter, passages that in my memory might've been one block paragraph, ten pages, like something from Beckett's *Molloy*, the meticulous counting of stones for a bum transmuted onto this aging, reclusive writer cleaning dust, hair, various bodily effluvia from this dying piece of technology he clings to because it's allowed him this ability to render meaning, to figure something out. Because, it seems, Writer devoted himself to this kind of work in rendering all of it sensible, we can by extension witness these sensations through his texts—of looking, of poring, of fixating—thus allowing the experience to become a kind of Open Work, per Umberto Eco, wherein we complete the text in our reading, our identification, our own grown and growing obsession.

👁 👁 CONT'D: Writer once wrote a piece called "Notes Toward a Definitive Meditation (By Someone Else) on the Novel 'Americana' for *Epoch* Magazine, in 1972, speaking to qualities in the book, pretending an outsider's perspective:

> Within the central narrative, the action moves forward while the protag's camera looks back, at least most of the time.

Eventually it becomes clear (or almost clear) that the book is being "written" in the year 1999. The narrator-protagonist is living on a small island where he contemplates his celluloid adventures as a young man. He uses as source material not only his mental recollections of that period but the movie he began making while traveling west and finished during a period of time merely alluded to in the book. The time frame narrows and widens from 1999 to the 1960's, from island to continent, from movie-being-made to the events which inspired the movie."[15]

[15] "Notes Toward a Definitive Meditation (By Someone Else) on the Novel 'Americana'" for *Epoch* in 1972 (Vol 21, No. 3, pp. 327-329).

👁 👁 There seemed to exist even in the writers preceding Writer's generation a temptation to look at least a bit into the future when possible, situating their novels slightly at a remove from the present. Some of this seemed to stem from the aftermath of WWII, the anxiety around the Bomb, and the sense that worldwide catastrophe had only slightly been averted. For writers in the '60s and '70s, with media growing rampant, and culture suddenly cranked up to a level unprecedented at any point in history, this future orientation could often feel crazed, either in the work of figures like Philip K. Dick, more situatable in genre contexts, but markedly more frenetic and line-by-line bizarre than any of his forebears or contemporaries—and, weirdly, Dick grew more autobiographical with time, such that the future-orientation of *Valis*, e.g., as well as the language, and the preoccupation with a kind of American, idol-fixated spirituality almost feels closer to Writer's work than contemporaneous SF. There is future orientation, too, either in terms of representation of alternate reads on history—i.e., speculating about possible futures by reworking accepted versions of the past—as well as more direct futurity in writers like Barth, Barthelme, Coover, Ozick, and others writing around the time *Americana* comes out, though for Writer the device feels less about considering the possibilities of what a future world might hold, either for us, or for Bell in his fictional context, and more about the setup of this scenario wherein someone has sort of twinned the paths of their life, both on film, and in their actual experience, and offering potential commentary or observation on this strange phenomenon. As is indicated by the piece in *Epoch*, it's an element of the novel that feels *almost* clear, and probably less essential to the experience of reading it than following the language more intuitively, but the aspect of the home video camera is undeniable, the aspect of the eye as a new and vital utility for documenting one's history, for making sense of the whole of one's life, resounds upon reading, and feels as though it permeates the rest of the book even before we've reached this section, this preoccupation Bell has with both observing his surroundings and with documenting them, his eyes a sort of extended appendage in the form of the camera, becoming as smartphones now seem to be an object for keeping up with the movement of the modern world.

👁 👁 No art hung on the wall facing the Mao, so I went to lean against it and slowly slid down, looking up and taking it in. I've only come to understand Warhol's side of it now, but at the time I felt a great religiousness to the painting. It seemed like a revered thing. It had to be, it was taking up this massive space, this carved out corner in Chicago, awash in light, surrounded by the grays of the outside world. Warhol's religiousness is something I now take great comfort from, his daily, sometimes multiple-times daily attendances at church, the relative abstinence with which he approached most aspects of his life. At the time, though, any sense of the image I was then feeling was entirely due to Writer. *Mao II*, and the novel to follow it in Writer's 1990s work, *Underworld*, might in fact be called the most spiritual books he's produced. The former's opening, with the mass wedding under the Unification Church Blessing Ceremony, and the latter's bookended structure, split by two miraculous events. My sense of Warhol's image, then, was guided by my reading of Writer's novel, and enhanced a hundredfold by it. As I sifted in preparation for this work through contemporaneous reactions to Writer, simply to see what people made of the strangeness of this developing voice, as it seemed to move further and further from comprehensibility, I came to witness again the inevitable destructive force book reviewing can have on our initial reactions to a writer's work. I am not saying that book reviewers should not do what they do. I am grateful to the book reviewer. I simply think that there are things they can do, and things that they cannot do, and when Writer moves from *Americana* to *End Zone*, there would seem to be a really substantial disregard of expectation, of establishing a recognizable career in 1970s novelist terms, or probably any era's "novelist terms". Those sympathetic to Writer's endeavor—mostly writers themselves, like Joyce Carol Oates, Nelson Algren, Margo Jefferson, even John Updike—are happy to linger over his language, his rendering of the recognizable tableaux of 20th-century noveldom, i.e. New York City, marriages, political violence, athletic spectacle, etc. etc. etc., and praise his apparent disregard for the conventional constraints of plotting, character-development, or the dominant novelistic mode in the 70s, which isn't all that different from the dominant filmic mode in the American 70s. This is a great irony I'm facing, that literature en masse *did* become more filmic through the sixties, through the seventies, as a rule. Even Richard Brautigan could be said to have enacted a kind of Pop Art/Minimalist advertising spoof in early works like *Trout Fishing in America*; but in Writer, the idea of reflecting a TV-obsessed culture in the early work seems beyond banal, the notion of writing even a brilliant NYC screenplay readymade like *Looking for Mr. Goodbar* seems almost offensive when we see the areas wherein he's *actually* satirical—as in *Great Jones Street,* inventing rock mythology and lyric and more, or *White Noise,* regurgitating suburban academe tropes into the TV saturated populace via a cloud of toxic, unknown smoke that seeps out in grocery store jargon and Hitler obsession—or actually giving us a capacious, open cityscape like that of *Running Dog.* As I sat there, though, in the museum, back before this work existed even in thought, and back before I'd even begun to consider the rest of his texts, I felt the language coursing through me as I looked, and felt this sure connection between whatever Eye had made *Mao II* and Warhol's Eye, and the sense that I had thus far missed out on a great deal in not considering either of them, that there were things, forces, at play in American art and writing I'd probably mistakenly only attributed to the film and literature I'd read from Europe, the art I'd seen from Europe. I am lucky to be speaking largely retrospectively of his career, of course, to be able to see the tendrils and connectivities now that he's far along in age. The book reviewer operates entirely zoomed in, thinking of things a reader probably never thinks about, excepting under the advisement of the poor book reviewer. I wouldn't describe the experience of looking up at that artwork as terror, but certainly "awe," as I felt my consciousness slowing down, the room simplifying, my life in turn simplifying. There will often be talk, especially on the internet, of books changing people's lives. There's skepticism around it, as there is with anything seemingly grand, artful, potentially extreme or excessive. It isn't something I've ever questioned, because although it's become rarer the older I've gotten, I doubt if I'd have kept on writing and seeking out writers like Writer were it not for reading experiences that seemed as though they changed me, or in turn experiences of art that seemed to change me. That moment, I'm certain, would not have happened had I not read, and gotten entirely captivated by, *Mao II.* The entire spectacle of it seemed to wash over me, to course through me, somehow transmitted via its language such that it could affect me at a physiological level.

👁 👁 With the generalized separation of the Writer and his Works, every uniform view of successful activity and all direct engagement between himself and his audience are lost. Accompanying the articulation of a corpus, a body of work, and the focusing of their production process, unity or uniformity and communication have become the domain of the reviewer, the commentor, the publishing apparatus. The success of the publishing industry is the marginalization of the Writer, his or her Eye, and his or her Works.[16]

[16] "With the generalized separation of the worker and his products, every unitary view of accomplished activity and all direct personal communication among producers are lost. Accompanying the progress of accumulation of separate products and the concentration of the productive process, unity and communication become the exclusive attribute of the system's management. The success of the economic system of separation is the proletarianization of the world." (Debord). This is, of course, an unconscionable offense to mankind. Everywhere the middlemen of every industry are working to obfuscate the sure communication of the human spirit into the brainstem of all beings. These acts of separation. These pathetic acts of separation—even here, even this, surely I'm guilty of it too. "The perturbations, anxieties, depravations, deaths, exceptions in the physical or moral order, spirit of negation, brutishness, hallucinations fostered by the will, torments, destruction, confusion, tears, insatiabilities, servitudes, delving imaginations, novels, the unexpected, the forbidden, the chemical singularities of the mysterious vulture which lies in wait for the carrion of some dead illusion, precocious & abortive experiences, the darkness of the mailed bug, the terrible monomania of pride, the inoculation of deep stupor, funeral orations, desires, betrayals, tyrannies, impieties, irritations, acrimonies, aggressive insults, madness, temper, reasoned terrors, strange inquietudes which the reader would prefer not to experience , cants, nervous disorders, bleeding ordeals that drive logic at bay, exaggerations, the absence of sincerity, bores, platitudes, the somber, the lugubrious, childbirths worse than murders, passions, romancers at the Courts of Assize, tragedies,-odes, melodramas, extremes forever presented, reason hissed at with impunity, odor of hens steeped in water, nausea, frogs, devilfish, sharks, simoon of the deserts, that which is somnambulistic, squint-eyed, nocturnal, somniferous, noctambulistic, viscous, equivocal, consumptive, spasmodic, aphrodisiac, anemic, one-eyed, hermaphroditic, bastard, albino, pederast, phenomena of the aquarium, & the bearded woman, hours surfeited with gloomy discouragement, fantasies, acrimonies, monsters, demoralizing syllogisms, ordure, that which does not think like a child, desolation, the intellectual manchineel trees, perfumed cankers, stalks of the camellias, the guilt of a writer rolling down the slope of nothingness & scorning himself with joyous cries, that grind one in their imperceptible gearing, the serious spittles on inviolate maxims, vermin & their insinuating titillations, stupid prefaces like those of Cromwell, Mademoiselle de Maupin & Dumas fils, decaying, helplessness, blasphemies, suffocation, stifling, mania,--before these unclean charnel houses, which I blush to name, it is at last time to react against whatever disgusts us & bows us down." — Lautréamont, *Chants de Maldoror.*

👁 👁 CONT'D SPECTACLE IN *END ZONE*: "IT'S NOT EASY to fake a limp. The tendency is to exaggerate, a natural mistake and one that no coach would fail to recognize. Over the years I had learned to eliminate this tendency. I had mastered the dip and grimace, perfected the semi-moan, and when I came off the field this time, after receiving a mild blow on the right calf, nobody considered pressing me back into service. The trainer handed me an ice pack and I sat on the bench next to Bing Jackmin, who kicked field goals and extra points. The practice field was miserably hot. I was relieved to be off and slightly surprised that I felt guilty about it. Bing Jackmin was wearing headgear; his eyes, deep inside the facemask, seemed crazed by sun or dust or inner visions.

"Work," he shouted past me. "Work, you substandard industrial robots. Work, work, work, work."

"Look at them hit," I said. "What a pretty sight. When Coach says hit, we hit. It's so simple."

"It's not simple, Gary. Reality is constantly being interrupted. We're hardly even aware of it when we're out there. We perform like things with metal claws. But there's the other element. For lack of a better term I call it the psychomythical. That's a phrase I coined myself."

"I don't like it. What does it refer to?"

"Ancient warriorship," he said. "Cults devoted to pagan forms of technology. What we do out on that field harks back. It harks back. Why don't you like the term?"

"It's vague and pretentious. It means nothing. There's only one good thing about it. Nobody could remember a stupid phrase like that for more than five seconds. See, I've already forgotten it."

"Wuuurrrrk. Wuuuurrrrrk."

EZ, 35-36

👁 👁 As opposed to opening *End Zone* with a more relaxed language and then supplementing the rest of this topic-specific novel with specialized language around college football, Writer's impulse is to include a great deal of the former, and embrace the particular strain of his own language-generating apparatus (head) to extract the weird, alien-like observer qualities of *Americana*, and many of his other texts—I am not interested in writing of his progression any further, and that isn't why I'm referring again to *End Zone*; I am interested mainly in snatches of his text that have drawn my attention along the strictures established for this work—and the net effect is, as evident, a kind of hilarity only really accessible when someone with an entirely unique perspective on almost everything presents their thinking cleanly, without considering convention, story, character, any of it; he speaks directly to us from the inside of his skull. There really aren't people raising questions or approaching the subject of football along these lines, even still. "Ancient warriorship," [...] "Cults devoted to pagan forms of technology." [...] And the sentence preceding it, that seemingly impossibly begins with the phrase Bing Jackmin was wearing headgear: "Bing Jackmin was wearing headgear; his eyes, deep inside the facemask, seemed crazed by sun or dust or inner visions." What I mean to say is that any writer functions as a kind of mediator between the world and the eventual text. They are the thing that processes the world, and then inputs their sense of both their internal experience and the world as anybody does, and what they're able to bring together in this amounts to more—in the case of the novel, and the writer of any kind of fiction—than summoning "story" or "characters" from their imagination. Writer is a curator of experience, bringing together what is most ideally interesting to bear in his texts, whether formless or structured, and here has tapped into a strain of absurdism that he can treat straightly, ignoring fireworks and letting the weird spectacle of American existence live.

👁 👁 THE CRITIC'S EYE: Anthony Burgess's "No Health Anywhere" continues the tradition (started, at least, by Nelson Algren) of reacting to Writer in filmic terms:

"The naiveté of this American picture, itself a symptom of post-Vietnam shock, is belied by the sophistication of DeLillo's verbal technique. The cutting is as rapid as that found in Eisenstein's *October* and often as confusing: With so little delineation of either character or mise en scène, things tend to run together, as in a dropped bag of rotten fruit. I came to *Running Dog* after a re-read of Mann's *Doctor Faustus* - a more terrible picture of evil, since in that book evil corrupts the good - and found DeLillo's work a refresher course in the readjustment to contemporary literary values. There is something of Pynchon in it, and a little of John Hawkes. DeLillo has his own voice, harsh, eroded, disturbingly eloquent."[17]

[17] *Saturday Review*: September 16, 1978 - "No Health Anywhere" review of *Running Dog* by Anthony Burgess, p. 38.

👁 👁 What's notable is there's very little in Writer's work by the time of *Running Dog* to consider him the "cinema" novelist or anything. He doesn't write much about film, and if he does, it's most often in the manner of the Burt Lancaster stuff in *Americana.* In *Running Dog,* the films referenced are mostly in the context of the art world, and in anticipation of the film in Hitler's bunker, but it's not as if he's writing about Old Hollywood or something. He's mostly writing about people, and the scenes included already from *Running Dog* are indicative of much of the movement of the text, scene-to-scene, darkness and light, conversation, a building paranoia. It isn't as if he's even making the references we get to Eisenstein himself *Underworld*, and even then, the apparatus of the film is more a way of moving throughout the crowd and further commentary on shadows and light than something like Theodore Roszak's brilliant *Flicker.* Subject matter always feels sort of secondary with Writer, much in the way we might say the particularities of philosophy are sort of secondary in much of Wittgenstein, meaning the actual particulars, subfields and that kind of thing. The thing of interest is the "verbal technique" in Writer, because that's what's going to give shape to these works, for him and for us. Further, there's something warm in seeing two avowed Joyceans, on opposite sides of the Atlantic, sort of communing in this way. Notable, too, given Joyce's persistent interest in film, and Burgess's justifiably strange relationship to the medium after a slim novel he wrote got adapted and dwarfed the rest of his career. There is, too, a luring temptation to read in the Writer's work, should it span as Writer's does, a kind of (fictional) (secret) history of the twentieth and the early twenty-first centuries. The writer in any capacity is concerned with processing, with rendering and with making sense of *something*, be it only language for the Poet, history for the Biographer, experience for the Autofictionist, or some variation of each of these and more for the mere writer, for Writer as for countless others in his mode. The Writer has processed, in this case, the Warren Commission Report on the assassination of John Fitzgerald Kennedy, New York City from 1950 to 2002, at least, a contemporaneous understanding of the incredibly complicated world of college football, and more and more and still more. The Writer, in this case, has eaten time, and eaten the sights and sounds of our moments, our America, not merely to offer back "the news that stays news," (Pound, *ABCs of Reading*) but the burrowing language of our offending society, its spectacle, our societyspectacle horrorshow, its redolence, its beauty, its impossible mountains of trash, *to consider,* irradiated, in lines of text upon our screens or pages on our trains, in our beds, on our couches, the Writer offers this.

👁 👁 I no longer remember what I read the night before, no matter what it is, no matter how long I read, no matter how immersed I might've felt. I'm not the kind of person to annotate the books I read, whether on Kindle, iPhone, or in print on a page. I've tried it, and it just isn't really for me. I've seen images of the books of people who do this, and there are some of them I admire, even aspire to, but any time I've tried to do it I just don't feel like my natural self. It's important for a person reading to feel like their natural self. It's important to feel like they're being honest with themselves. People often lie to themselves about their reading, their comprehension, and what's important. I know this because I do it constantly. In the grand scheme of things I'm not a *good reader*, per Nabokov. I didn't really arrive at writing solely out of a love of literature. I didn't have the romantic childhood experience of reading as many writers do. There are writers I admire who didn't have this. Writer, actually, seems to be just such a person. The other night I watched an interview with Salman Rushdie wherein he talked about a memory of V.S. Naipaul at a conference being asked about his perspective as a reader, to which he replied "I am a *writer*, not a reader." What's interesting is, Umberto Eco is quoted in the Guardian as having said the *exact* same thing, years ago. It seems unlikely, though not impossible, that Rushdie could've mistaken Naipaul and Eco. If you were to pick, for instance, two random paragraphs from either writer, I might struggle to tell you who's who, not knowing much Naipaul myself, but knowing a good bit of Eco—i.e., not all that much—but in terms of their physical forms, while certainly similar in terms of their gutly rotundity, could hardly be mistaken. A quick search revealed no such quotation from Naipaul. A quick search revealed precisely the same quote from Umberto Eco. Rushdie, for his part, is not *bad*, of course, for thinking in this manner. It simply means that Rushdie *did* arrive at writing from a love of literature, or more particularly a love of reading. I can't be sure whether it matters, but for whatever it's worth I've never particularly enjoyed reading Rushdie, whereas I've loved Eco, and I've loved, too, Writer, who although he hasn't overtly said something like "I'm a writer not a reader," has certainly explored the notion of being influenced by other sources *than* mere literature, mere reading, and at the very least it is important to me, to readers and writers like me, to have figures like this, both in terms of their commentary on these matters, and in terms of their actual work, since in the case of either Eco or Writer, their sense of *needing more*, perhaps, of seeking to *contain more* than a reflection of one's mere love of reading, within one's texts, conveyed by them, can allow a reader, let's say, perhaps ashamedly, perhaps cringedly ashamedly, a *modern reader*, to access the wonderment of reading that speaks right to them, that even welcomes them, that lets them in.

👁 👁 MORE SPECTACLE *END ZONE*: "What you were saying earlier about what scares you. Where the true danger is. Something about patriotic manifestations."

"Let me just simply mention flag-waving and the insane repetitive ritualizing that goes on every time a flag is hiked up a pole or some veterans of Gettysburg come hobbling along with their medals, their stickpins, their poppies, their flags, their hats, their banners, their bumper stickers, or some simple sports event where you look up suddenly and there's sixteen thousand Shriners and Masons with their comical Turkish hats and they're covering every inch of the playing field with, in the middle of them all, three hundred and eighty-five high school girls dressed in red, white and blue who are prostrating themselves on the cold earth as they assume the shape of an American flag being dragged through yak dung by syphilitic foreign students and off to the side there's some crippled television personality in a wheelchair and pulleys singing the national anthem as the cystic fibrosis child of the month poses in the nude for the cover of Life. I tend to worry about such spectacles."

EZ, 164

👁 👁 This is a pure and a righteous anger. It would hopefully be apparent to any reading this that there is a strain of both righteous and pure anger running throughout this book, and this section. It is quite beautiful to witness this anger. We can understand, sure, sure, Writer's varied relationship with sport. He does love it, we can probably infer, but like anyone given to thinking hard about much of their existence, he doesn't seem capable of letting himself wholly love it, and thus he begins interrogating the dimensions of it that are, in fact, not particularly lovable, and does it so angrily, ripping into the spectacle, showing us this ugly and dumb and silly spectacle there on the field, before the game or during the half time show, whenever they do it. He is doing Debord's work. Here, the Writer's sense of the language on the page is important, as it too is a part of the imagery of the world, the visualization process apparent in his work. In a letter to David Foster Wallace, who's elsewhere talked about how the Writer highlighted the words on the page to him, the Writer writes of "a sensitivity to the actual appearance of words on a page, to letter-shapes and letter-combinations. In a line you quote--snow that was drilled and gilded with dog piss--there is the assonance of "drilled" and "gilded" but also the particular shaping nature of the letters "i" and "l" and "d" in "drilled and gilded" and the sort of visual echo of the "i" in "piss" at the end of the line. And the "o" sound of "dog" and "snow" tend to mate these words in my eyes and mind). These are round words, as it were, and the others are slim or i-beamed or tall or whatever."[18][19] Because any writer is inevitably bound to writing as the means of getting their work done—which, duh, but beyond this the notion of actually shaping one's whole perception towards the work, i.e. one's senses, in an intuitive way rather than an intellectual one (his descriptors or way of characterizing the method is simple, referring to letters, because clearly the playing of the notes is the thing)—even his sense of individual letters is bound up in this process of looking, of paying attention to the structures apparent within the world, of trying to make sense of living when there's just so much of it happening everywhere, at any given moment. One could say this pretty easily of any page of Writer's writing, which is comforting. It is comforting to have a method. The method must change as the person

18 http://kottke.org.s3.amazonaws.com/dfw/DFW-DD.pdf

19 The line being referenced comes from *Underworld*, and is exquisite, and is as follows: "Bleak and weedy streets, unshoveled snow going grim with bus exhaust, snow that was drilled and gilded with dog piss, and there were usually a few lurking figures in green fatigues, the last of a straggle battalion of wasted men."

changes, but the change is not one of scrapping everything and starting anew, unless it really really is, in the case of maybe Joyce, kind of, but mostly it's sculpture, starting with something quite large, a slab of marble, and ending one's life writing with the perfect autoportrait in stone. It is such a pure and such a righteous pure anger that I happen to love.

👁 👁 THE EYE IN *THE SILENCE:* "When everyone was seated, here, there, the newcomers spoke of the flight and the events that followed and the spectacle of the midtown streets, the grid system, all emptied out.

"In darkness."

"No street lights, store lights, high-rise buildings, skyscrapers, all windows everywhere."

"Dark."

TS, 70

👁 👁 As with *Point Omega*, I'm particularly interested in *The Silence* because it seems to adapt and update Writer's impulses to the current moment, not in an attempt to pander, since Writer really hasn't done much, if any, of that throughout his career, but in the interest of advancing the form of the novel in Writer's lifetime, and really by this I mean advancing the form of fiction, and really by this I mean advancing the writing itself, and by this language. In *Point Omega,* the energy is devoted to slowness, but in a compressed space, considering the landscape, and art, and the interactions of same; advancing, then, by considering the phenomenon of slowness, sort of recurring from the time of Antonioni, who Writer started with, in the work of artists like Douglas Gordon, and by extension interests in slow cinema, culture, etc. With *The Silence*, the adaptation and updating of Writer's impulses, and the effort towards advancing language, writing, fiction, the novel, is far more at the level of form, stripping away anything unnecessary, not so much compressing as chipping away at the stones of Writer's earlier works, such that it's practically short enough to be memorizable. What's interesting, too, is that the prior spectacles of the twentieth century, the bright lights, the gun flashes, the explosions, the films, the football games, the baseball games, are inverted in *The Silence*; the spectacle is now the absence, the sudden darkness of the streets, the quieting of the electrical grid, the deadness of every phone. It registers as that here, but over the course of the novel it's almost as if we undergo a kind of detox, the world so stripped of its lights and attractions that we are simply human once again, unattached, monastic, alone in the universe. Some of this, too, I think has to do with the quickness with which one can read *The Silence*. Other writers, Derek McCormack, Thomas Moore, Dennis Cooper, have long been embracing this lean into concision, to saying less, making the experience of reading their works, just like *The Silence*, more visceral, more immersive and sensory, and more contemporary. It isn't the only possible way for a modern writer to reach their readers—and really, the general critical assessment of *The Silence* was lukewarm, indicating this method's still in progress—but it's one that feels as extreme as the late period shift of David Markson, shedding the prior decade's tendency towards length, and using the way of being in the modern world that feels perhaps initially less overtly "literary," but far more brilliant and entrancing.

👁 👁 This project began as an attempt to think only about *Mao II*, because it's a novel I return to frequently in my thinking about what the novel itself as a form, or fiction generally, can do. It wasn't thematic, and it wasn't necessarily just his use of language. Slowly this pattern started to take shape. A pattern not exactly extracted so much as a pattern recognized in me, in what I'd resonated with, in moments in interviews that gave me pause, and in a sense of fear about death. I'd read that list of title ideas someone shared from Writer's papers at the Harry Ransom Center in Texas for *White Noise*. *Panasonic* was one, *Mein Kampf* was another. I opened the book and tried to find sections apparently cribbed directly from advertising, from billboards, from radio, from TV. I was looking at things I'd seen in the world around me. Toyota Celicas. White noise machines. Panasonic products. Advertising speak from plastered-over posters outside coffee shops or in grocery stores. These weren't just evocative titles for their own linguistic uniqueness, i.e. *just his use of language*—an aspect of writing I find I'm having to stop myself from only thinking of for fear of losing my sense of anything much larger than a sentence with any sustenance, a fate which is not probably too awful. They were also visual things. Sculptural things. I can't see the word *Panasonic* without picturing a TV set. The black bar along the bottom and the bulbous glass screen poking out above it like an alien's black gut. The words themselves took on this visual weight, and then I got thinking about things he'd describe, often cleanly, without excessive ornamentations to attach them to people, or if they were people then they were often rendered strangely, with descriptors that often felt alien, like the TV's glass gut. I thought, too, of the covers. Of Chairman Mao's face plastered over *Mao II*. Of the church reaching up towards the skyscraper behind it, awash in overcast sky, on *Underworld*. Of Lee Harvey Oswald posing with a rifle, small and simple, surrounded by an otherwise average-looking paperback one might see on an airport thriller, the mass market paperback I'd bought of *Libra*. As *Libra* illustrates, the act of looking is now, and may forever be, a charged thing in contemporary life. It is exploding the first real event to glue millions of eyes to the TV set for hours, days even. What we get from Writer of course isn't *only* looking, but the amount of focus he puts on it across every single thing he's written provides us a means of processing life that seems to speak finally to why people wind up reading novels at all. I couldn't find the quote when looking, but somewhere, maybe in a review, I remember someone talking about Proust. The idea was that there's some art that can make you look twice at your own life, and that this might be one of the better things art can provide for us. Like Godard for Writer, and Godard/Antonioni/etc. for countless men and women in the 60s, 70s, 80s, and through to today. The best art might not be a hammer over the head in the name of an author's perspective, but a curious blend, a way of seeing, that allows us to observe our world anew. Proust himself talked about seeing with new eyes, and Proust's own relationship to the work of John Ruskin—a writer on art, who Proust credited, in a manner similar to Writer and Godard/Antonioni/etc., when one considers citing the influence of a critic on perhaps the world's greatest autobiographical novelist compared with, say, another great autobiographical novelist, or even a novelist—seems testimony to an awareness of this as one of, if not *the* ideal goal, for an artist in any medium, but probably especially a novelist. To *look again*, to see the world, but not only the world, but *the world within the world*; this would seem to be Writer's mission, his overarching light, across all of his work. Because of this I feel justified in not trying to give a summation of all of his work. I don't know what that might offer that a Wikipedia entry could not. Instead, I'm looking to the images, to where he looks, where his characters look, and what he and his characters look at. I've attempted to be meticulous, but have not attempted to point to every single instance of the looker and the looked-at; that isn't the goal. The goal is to understand how this is one of the significant ways of viewing the work of one of the most significant American writers of the late twentieth and turn of the twenty-first centuries. Because his work has meant so much to me, and informed me, and because through it I do see a hope and a necessary warping towards that hope for writing fiction of an all-encompassing, life-wide sort. When I think of Proust, I am most captivated by the idea that he could see in an art critic/essayist a method that might serve him in exploding the minutia of his childhood life into a massive, exhaustive sequence of autobiographical fiction. When I think of Writer, I am most captivated by this notion of the eye.

👁 👁 I am invested in saying something in this work about the nature of reading, not dissimilar to Nicholas Branch's apparent desire to construct a kind of secret history in looking. Reading has always been a loaded endeavor, for me, not something I necessarily went into idly or lightly, but something I went into searching for a kind of secret history, or larger truth, and a guide for how I might approach writing in my own life. Writer has been a figure on that journey, more or less the entire way, so I'm approaching this work in a manner I think is befitting this kind of thinking. He's a part of it, and a part of me, and a part of my understanding of why people read and write novels, and yet I don't exactly understand the mechanics, or rather the mechanism; and while I'm not necessarily certain it's my ambition to understand it, I do view it as certainly as worthwhile as devoting myself to, say, an analysis of graffiti throughout Writer's novels, or an analysis of sociopolitical conditions during the Cold War informing his Middle Period, etc. etc. I'm also influenced here by the novelist, academic, and critic Nicholas Rombes. On his own, Nick published a book called *10/40/70*, wherein he allows himself to write about the tenth, fortieth, and seventieth minutes of various films, and expounds his own ideas on why this seemed a sensible approach for the critic in the present day. I'm interested in constraint in my own fiction and criticism, and I'm approaching my work with this in mind. When I personally looked at the whole of Writer's works, that notion is what kept resonating for me. The eye. The people staring at screens. At artworks. At strangers on the street. He gave me something, something I hold dearly. When I went searching within myself for a logical constraint, then, the eye guided me. What I've got, then, is this assemblage of images, returning hopefully to the origins of this Writer, the world he was observing in movie theaters and on pages and throughout the life he observed, and continues to observe. What I don't have is a study of "image," or a critical-theoretical treatise. I distrust absolute certainty most of all in criticism, so I don't aspire to it and I don't even necessarily hope to articulate an authority in writing this way. I have no authority, not on Writer or anyone else. In fact, it's this that's informed my choice in referring to him as "Writer" herein the majority of the time, not as a gesture of disrespect to him, but rather a gesture of expressing a lack of expertise, authority, absolute knowledge or even familiarity from me. I am dumb, and better at lying than I am at doing serious work, academic work, the reading, the poring, the focusing. He is Writer, then, because he represents a certain ideal I don't feel conversant with, and also because I love him, and view him as a kind of transitional figure in our present, an ur-Writer for those of us who face a hopelessness and a fear we don't know how to deal with. To find out, for instance, that Writer told Harold Brodkey at one point to "watch more television," that Brodkey was terribly freaked out, and that Writer said this—to me, that is a thing as pure as anything in Plato's Republic, as any other ideal form.[20] I don't feel capable of the kind of work done by figures like Gilles Deleuze, though I am interested in it. I don't feel interested in or capable of the kind of criticism that writes off, whole cloth, particular eras in a writer's career—pre- and post-*Underworld* being the most common in Writer's case. I do believe in criticism, however, in the critical impulse, be it from an admiring fellow fiction writer or someone analyzing something they have no interest in ever making at all. This is, then, in that spirit, drawing out this notion of seeing, of vision, throughout Writer, whose first novel was once characterized by Vince Passaro as "a television network programmer who hits the road in search of the big picture," a phrase not too far from articulating Writer's own journey as an artist, and finally, as a seer.

[20] Of course I'm aware of the ways in which this shrug is also a kind of copout, a way of eliding the fact that I actually am inexpert in certain things, but have also kind of performed as if I am, throughout here, and feel ashamed of this. I apologize, in either case, by including this footnote, for instance, here.

"The woman at the table was speaking about great human spectacles, the white-clad faithful in Mecca, the hadj, mass devotion, millions, year after year, and Hindus gathered on the banks of the Ganges, millions, tens of millions, a festival of immortality." [...] "I kept looking straight ahead, looking and thinking. The fact that these individuals, these heralds, had chosen to be rendered dead well before their time. The fact that their bodies had been emptied of indispensable organs. The fact of containment, alignment, bodies set in assigned positions. Woman man woman. It occurred to me that these were humans as mannequins. I allowed myself to think of them as brainless objects playing out a reversal of the spectacle I'd encountered earlier—the mannequins hunched in their burial chamber, in hoods and robes. And now this freeze-frame of naked humans in pods." [...] "But I had to pause now, stop and look, because the screen in the ceiling began to lower and a series of images filled the width of the hallway.

People running, crowds of running men and women, they're closely packed and showing desperation, dozens, then hundreds, workpants, T-shirts, sweatshirts, shouldering each other, elbowing, looking dead ahead, the camera positioned slightly above, an angled shot, no cuts, tilts, pans. I back away instinctively. There's no soundtrack but it's almost possible to hear the mass pulse of breath and pounding feet. They're running on a surface barely visible beneath their crowded bodies. I see tennis shoes, ankle boots, sandals, there's a barefoot woman, a man in sneakers with undone laces flapping.

They keep on coming, trying to escape some dreadful spectacle or rumbling threat. I'm watching closely and trying to think into the action onscreen, the uniformity of it, the orderly deployment and steady pace that underlie the urgent scene. It begins to occur to me that I may be seeing the same running cluster repeatedly, shot and reshot, two dozen runners made to resemble several hundred, a flawless sleight of editing." [...] "The plane circled lower and the complex appeared to float up out of the earth. All around it the immense fever burn of ash and rock. The sandstorm was out there, more visibly now, dust rising in great dark swelling waves, only upright, rollers breaking vertically, a mile high, two miles, I had no idea, trying to work miles into kilometers, then trying to think of the word, in Arabic, that refers to such phenomena. This is what I do to defend myself against some spectacle of nature. Think of a word." [...] "He was naked on a slab, not a hair on his body. It was hard to connect the life and times of my father to this remote semblance. Had I ever thought of the human body and what a spectacle it is, the elemental force of it, my father's body, stripped of everything that might mark it as an individual life. It was a thing fallen into anonymity, all the normal responses dimming now. I did not turn away. I felt obliged to look. I wanted to be contemplative. And at some far point in my wired mind, I may have known a kind of weak redress, the satisfaction of the wronged boy." [...] "Here, there were no lives to think about or imagine. This was pure spectacle, a single entity, the bodies regal in their cryonic bearing. It was a form of visionary art, it was body art with broad implications."

ZK, 62, 144, 151, 230, 250, 255

👁 👁 There are these statements throughout all of Writer's novels about Writer's sense of the functionality of the writer more generally. Here, there's this unique kind of applied looking, where not only is someone observing something—varied scenes of human tragedy—but they are trying to process it in a way that's highly personal, and yet somehow geared towards use, towards a kind of processing, "I'm watching closely and trying to think into the action onscreen," statements like this abound throughout his novels, *trying to think into the action* indicates a view of looking that feels mystical, especially surrounded as it is with these scenes of mass rituals, spectacles of the hadj at Mecca, as well as this preoccupation in turn with the word, with thinking of the Arabic word for something, another tendency running throughout Writer's work, i.e., how to take one's sense of something and render it, distill it. *The Silence* opens with a man on a plane doing just that, processing words and working with his wife to recall definitions. These late books not only provide a kind of Writer redux lens on his whole career, they function like crystallizations of that career, prisms through which we can re-view either the preceding works or fiction/writing thereafter. I bear witness, I think of a word for what I've seen, Writer seems to be suggesting. I let myself get drawn into what seems almost incomprehensible in terms of the ancient apparatus at hand, language, and all the same I try and express it. Just as the early years of writing were informed by what was printed—i.e., The Bible, and little else—the work of writers has consistently been to adapt to the textual environment one is given in one's lifetime. If industrialization gave John Dos Passos the means to write sort of automatically, almost shamanistically of the newspaper, the telegram, the radio, then the widespread saturation of the media landscape, the glowing screens of Times Square, the ubiquity of film culture gave writers new matter to contend with. For most this is viewed as an *oppositional* question, i.e., what might be done by writers to *fight* the ubiquity of images, of visual culture. For Writer, it's instead viewed as a *complementary* matter, i.e., this is the context I exist within, and thus it is incumbent on me to write *of* it, with it, and against it, which is not to say one is taking sides, but rather that we can advance the form only by pressing ourselves to and through our context, existing in relation to it.

◉ ◉ WHAT ARE THE QUESTIONS WRITERS ARE ASKING, OR OUGHT TO ASK, AT THE END OF THE TWENTIETH AND THE BEGINNING OF THE TWENTY FIRST CENTURY? WHAT WILL WE DO WHEN WRITER DIES? WHAT MIGHT A NOVELIST IN THE 1970S IN AMERICA COMMENT UPON IN THE NOVELISTS OF THE 50S AND 60S WITHOUT BORING EVERYONE CONCERNED STIFF? WELL WHAT ELSE IS THERE? WHAT OTHER ENTITIES MAKE UP THE WRITER'S CONTEXT?

👁 👁 "Nicholas Branch in his glove-leather armchair is a retired senior analyst of the Central Intelligence Agency, hired on contract to write the secret history of the assassination of President Kennedy. Six point nine seconds of heat and light. Let's call a meeting to analyze the blur. Let's devote our lives to understanding this moment, separating the elements of each crowded second. We will build theories that gleam like jade idols, intriguing systems of assumption, four-faced, graceful. We will follow the bullet trajectories backwards to their lives that occupy the shadows, actual men who moan in their dreams. Elm Street. A woman wonders why she is sitting on the grass, bloodspray all around. Tenth street. A witness leaves her shoes on the hood of a bleeding policeman's car. A strangeness, Branch feels, that is almost holy. There is much here that is holy, an aberration in the heartland of the real. Let's regain our grip on things."

L, 15

COMMISSION EXHIBIT 398 - 125G

[21] Abraham Zapruder / Warren Commission, z230 from the Zapruder film.

👁 👁 For most novelists who've treated the subject of Oswald, of JFK's assassination, the interest is mostly devoted to Event, Incident, but these moments of retrospection in *Libra* feel far more "ecstatic," really, than the scenes exploring the actual events around this particular moment in history. Branch is maybe the perfect character for Writer, an observer, in an official capacity, freed up to wax philosophically and poetically about minutia in the home video footage of Abraham Zapruder. This, to me, seems to interest Writer most, or it feels the most charged when I think of my experiences reading *Libra* in various contexts throughout my life. It's ironic, because James Ellroy was directly inspired by reading *Libra* to write his treatment of the same events, *American Tabloid*, but in Ellroy's version we experience a far more "conventional," so to speak, exploration of what leads to the killing of JFK, and, in turn, the killing of Lee Harvey Oswald. Ellroy's novel is brilliant too, but it's brilliant in a pretty cinematic, wild, frenetic way, whereas Writer's *Libra* feels rather meditative in comparison, even the treatments of scenes of spycraft or actual violence or its implication feel part and parcel with Branch's digressions on shadows and light, time and death, and the knowing absurdity of this whole endeavor. In a way, it's as if Writer's interest is not so much in the original acts, the original experiences of life in his lifetime, as he is their representations, in Schopenhauerian terms, their *renderings*, much in the way he didn't conceive of some fictional treatment of the actual Baader-Meinhof terrorist group, or use "noirish" language to treat the "24 Hour Psycho" sections of *Point Omega*. It's an extrapolation of an extrapolation, and really we're probably better off reading the *Warren Commission Report* ourselves if our desire is to fully understand anything about JFK—among probably hundreds of other books, including those printed between the finishing of this sentence and the printing of this book—since, like Joyce's Dublin before him, any "real" stuff in Writer's books is best understood as a sort of prism through which to view and understand either Writer himself, or Writer's body of work in toto, which is as it should be. There are writers devoted to subject matter, and they will have their moments in the sun, but Writer, it seems, views subject matter as ancillary to his fundamental work, being the shaping of texts in language, and because he happens to live through this gigantic flood of imagery at the end of the 20th century, the things that give contexts for his shaping of texts are often those things we've seen, and seen, and seen again, working to enliven them and render them much in the manner of the humble American clothing manufacturer Abraham Zapruder.

👁 👁 And it is ascendant, the image, the watching; and reading, conversely, does seem to be descending, or let us not say descending, but it is *changing*, as is writing; but there's heart to be taken here from Writer, because where others have either inflected their work with frustration over this, abandoned ship, or attempted to incorporate actual visuals or strange text-visuals into their work, Writer's work has remained resolutely sentential, but in so doing has seemingly subsumed the image, the watching. He writes novels, primarily, and probably preferably. He's written plays, short stories, long novels, short novels, novellas, and in each of them he's figured out ways to utilize the world of the late twentieth and early twenty-first century that feel relatively untapped by most other writers, excepting those outspokenly or quietly influenced by Writer. Some have dug their heels firmly into an old way of writing, to varying degrees of success and interest. Pynchon, to an extent, embodies this. And let me say that I do not mean financial success when I say success. And I do not mean the interest of millions when I say interest. I mean only that the work be interesting, per James, and successful in terms of being written in this world, the modern world, and not as if TV never happened, smartphones never happened, and the techniques of Charles Dickens are perfectly suited to any moment's expression. Others have ripped up the form and opened the possibilities yet more. Markson, Robison, Renata Adler even. Writer's works, in turn, experiment—and weirdly he seems more comfortable in experimenting formally now, late in his career, though *Great Jones Street* is certainly as experimental as any contemporary novel in that vein I can think of. But what's so enchanting about Writer is I'm able to read it and simultaneously know Melville *and* reality television, I'm able to feel strange reverberations of Bob Dylan alongside episodes of *The Sopranos* or *Cops*; somehow, it's all in there, nothing's disregarded, I see it all.

👁 👁 JEAN-LUC GODARD ON THE WRITERS: "When you become older, the analysis of the structure is part of the novel itself. It's the difference between James Joyce's *Ulysses* and Erle Stanley Gardner. In *Perry Mason* the mystery is only the mystery of describing, [whereas with Joyce] the mystery of the writing itself is part of the novel. The observer and the universe are part of the same universe. It's what science discovered at the beginning of this century, when they say you can't tell where an atomic particle is. You know where they are, but not their speed; or you know their speed but not their place, because it depends on you. The one who describes is part of the description."[22]

[23]

[22] Rahman, Aninda. "Godard on the Modern Subject," n.d.
[23] Gary Stevens, Jean-Luc Godard at Berkeley, 1968.

👁 👁 Of course there is a big part of me that wishes Writer tried something on the order of *Histoires du Cinema*, or the more meta- films of Godard wherein he starts cannibalizing his own work and legacy, or the late work wherein things become extraordinarily simple, the scenes themselves simple, as in *Goodbye to Language*, but aspects of the technique, either with different approaches to technology, or scenario, or improvisation, are on the very cutting edge of filmmaking in any era. I can understand why Writer's works don't ever exactly do this—they don't fictionally treat the Writer's plight, they don't comment, really, on the state of fiction, or novels, or books, at least not directly—because these meta- approaches become their own kind of subject matter, as in the works of Barth, and can prove limiting when the vocal register or the pure image is really the thing. So it seems apparent that where Godard influenced Writer is certainly in the early work, and the influence would seem to have more to do with disruption, disorder, and attention to the eye than to a kind of playfulness that would be quite difficult to pull off in the novel form anyway. He is, however, drawing from the same well as Godard is here, allowing the text of his works to contain the figuring-out of themselves within them, not in terms of notes about his process, but in terms of framing his characters, and framing us, as readers, as detectives, rather than as entities with any stable sense of the world, its actors, and the context and ramifications for whatever we happen to be reading. One might, for instance, read *Libra* to solve the case, but of course in so doing one would feel a bit disappointed in that endeavor by novel's end. This is not because Writer doesn't know—probably he doesn't, but better-funded entities than Writer have seriously devoted far longer to the assassination of JFK and come away with a far murkier understanding than *Libra* communicates—but because he doesn't seem to be writing to know. Novelists who write to know, it should be said, are usually quite boring, and do better with plucked-from-the-headlines thrillers than the kind of work happening in *Libra*. He is wading into the *Warren Commission Report* to develop a kind of linguistic lens, a voice, a register, mining this exceptionally American document for its music, and then, like the goat in the old Mickey Mouse cartoon who eats sheet music and becomes a kind of instrument, rendering that music in the contained space of the novel to offer us something tangible, certainly, but concerned with a kind of reverberant truth, a mood-based truth, a vibration, which depending on our disposition will either send us further into the Oswald rabbit hole, or let us observe the continuation of American life inflected by this thing, or both.

👁 👁 MICHELANGELO ANTONIONI ON THE IMAGE AND *THE PASSENGER*: "**M.A.**: This was an idea that I had. Sometimes, I realized that I was following this same idea after the sequence was shot. This means that the idea was inside me and not theoretically formulated.

This is a film about someone who is following his destiny, a man watching reality as reported, in the same way that I was watching him, in the same way that you are pursuing me. You could go back and find another camera watching me and another one watching the other camera. It's surrealistic, isn't it?

R.E.: What hope is there to get beyond the images? We see countless photographs in the newspapers of mutilated bodies, of starving children. We hear the news repeated over and over again, every fifteen minutes on the radio. We titillate ourselves nightly with violence and commercials offered by television.

We are confronted in your film with an execution.

M.A.: This is a very ambiguous piece of film. Locke is doing a documentary film on a guerrilla movement within an African country. He is trying to get more and more politically involved. We can think that he chooses to shoot the execution because he knows that it will be visually impressive. He may have chosen to use it for sensationalism but perhaps not. We don't know, and perhaps he, himself, did not know what he wanted. I begin the sequence with a full screen as though it was happening that moment. And then we see it viewed by the television producer on the moviola for his documentary of David Locke's life as a journalist. This is another way that I was able to be free with my camera. I recorded the execution twice so that the audience's perception of that event would be different each time that they watched it. The format on the screen was different from the format on the moviola . It was as though I was filming the execution myself. And then it was watched by Knight and Rachel on the moviola as film shot by Locke."[24]

[24] Epstein, Renee, "Interview: Michelangelo Antonioni," *Film Comment Magazine*, 1975.

👁 👁 If the advent of the camera did in turn disrupt painting and bring about abstract expressionism, logic would follow that the invention of the camera might affect *all* art forms. First the text becomes reproducible, copyable, and then the text can be commented upon. The critique of the church by Martin Luther happens, for instance, on a piece of paper nailed to a door, just like the footage of JFK's assassination is pulled from home video footage of the president's appearance in Zapruder's city. The technology comes, and with it the preceding technology, and text is commented upon, enhanced, interrogated for all its worth—and probably beyond its worth, if we're honest. This attention, though, that Antonioni gives to the weird spiraling effect the camera has had, with one "camera watching me and another one watching the other camera," feels, really, like an observation that could just as easily come out of one of Writer's novels, or interviews, and *The Passenger*, not to mention most of Antonioni's post-1971 (i.e. post-*Americana*) work feels very much in line with where Writer's work has moved from its beginning.

👁 👁 WRITER ON FILM AND THE EYE: "Film allows us to examine ourselves in ways earlier societies could not—examine ourselves, imitate ourselves, extend ourselves, reshape our reality. It permeates our lives, this double vision, and also detaches us, turns some of us into actors doing walk-throughs. In my work, film and television are often linked with disaster. Because this is one of the energies that charges the culture. TV has a sort of panting lust for bad news and calamity as long as it is visual. We've reached the point where things exist so they can be filmed and played and replayed.... Think about the images most often repeated. The Rodney King videotape or the Challenger disaster or Ruby shooting Oswald. These are the images that connect us the way Betty Grable used to connect us in her white swimsuit, looking back at us over her shoulder in the famous pinup. And they play the tape again and again and again and again. This is the world narrative, so they play it until everyone in the world has seen it."[25]

[25] Don DeLillo, "The Art of Fiction," No. 135, *The Paris Review*, Fall 1993.

👁 👁 That the writer exists within the world, and their world is their plight, and their relationship with their plight will carry them through the slow days of their lives—these are perhaps obvious things, but when we encounter their books we are encountering them piecemeal, slowly, too, and often without the unifying threads typically afforded from career retrospectives. That the great gift, then, a writer might give a reader, in Proustian terms, could be to cause them not to look upon their works and feel such reverence, but that a reader could look twice upon their life and feel such reverence. Oddly, then, entirely apart from Proustian or Knausgaardian noticing, recounting, remembering, Writer is a sort of mirror, or better still a refracting device, letting us see through his seeing a present which has been called paranoiac, strange, crazed, violent, propulsive, et cetera ad infinitum; a present which is made of the text and the sights of our times. That the image is probably the primary corrupting device of our present, with most media outlets operating on this "sort of panting lust for bad news and calamity," we are lucky not only that Writer bothers investigating such a question as he goes about the writing, largely, of novels, but that these kinds of questions seem to inform the machinations of his work, especially so when we look from the trajectory from the Burt Lancaster fixation in *Americana*, through Oswald and the Zapruder film, through Warhol and Mao and "24 Hour Psycho" to finally the blackout—the "Silence," of the title, in its way, of course—it seems he's processing exactly what Antonioni was fixated on, where Wallace pinned down addiction, boredom, mental illness and their relationship to American life, consumerism, fulfillment as essential themes for modern work from the 80s through his suicide in 2008, Writer pinned down a problem of his time being on one hand the sheer power of the image, the repetition of the image, and the affecting of perspective and global mood by way of the selection of particular images worth repeating, or the instantaneous widespread circulation of images that are simply too fucked up not to grab one by their shirt.

👁 👁 THE EYE IN *AMERICANA*: "Quincy's wife and my date smiled at each other's peace earrings. Then I took B.G. into the living room. We waited for somebody to approach us and start a conversation. It was a party and we didn't want to talk to each other. The whole point was to separate for the evening and find exciting people to talk to and then at the very end to meet again and tell each other how terrible it had been and how glad we were to be together again. This is the essence of Western civilization. But it didn't matter really because an hour later we were all bored. It was one of those parties which are so boring that boredom itself soon becomes the main topic of conversation. One moves from group to group and hears the same sentence a dozen times. "It's like an Antonioni movie." But the faces were not quite as interesting."

A, 4

26

[26] Antonioni, Michelangelo, screenshot from *L'eclisse*. 1962.

👁 👁 *Life, friends, is boring. We must not say so.*
After all, the sky flashes, the great sea yearns,
we ourselves flash and yearn,
and moreover my mother told me as a boy
(repeatingly) 'Ever to confess you're bored
means you have no

Inner Resources.' I conclude now I have no
inner resources, because I am heavy bored.
Peoples bore me,
literature bores me, especially great literature,
Henry bores me, with his plights & gripes
as bad as achilles,

who loves people and valiant art, which bores me.[27]

We needn't say so. Boredom, per Wallace, can probably be transcended, can probably be made to flower into something more nourishing. Antonioni certainly feels, has felt, boring for me, as has every artist I deeply love. The question has to start to change. Boredom needn't be the death knell we started perceiving it to be in the later twentieth century. Boredom isn't uniformly bad. Boredom can be interesting. The other side of monotony, say, when working a dead-end job, and we start to become a bit delusional. We develop a system for sneaking off to the bathroom, say, when things become particularly hellish. We steal food, say, from the breakroom, because we're bored. We peruse the internet on company time. We stare at the clock. The problem is we've taken it in that boredom is the absolute enemy at all costs. In *Americana*, as in the many great texts of boredom, of slackerdom, at least comments on this boredom, injects it with something, with association, with feeling, with reference, thus enlivening it, lifting it up. Boredom, per Wallace, can exist just next to extreme focus, a state of Zen, which feels entirely in line with the Nicholas Branches of Writer's works, and though he killed himself before he could complete it, Wallace's *The Pale King* presents this kind of reworked boredom into a means of dealing with contemporary existence, with the modern world, much in the way the figure staring at the "Baader-Meinhof" paintings, or "24 Hour Psycho," or the party

[27] John Berryman, Dream Song 14 from *The Dream Songs*. Copyright © 1969 by John Berryman, renewed 1997 by Kate Donahue Berryman.

even in *Americana* have managed. But absent the mere recounting of one's boredoms, their stirrings—can we, for instance, tap into the other many bored writers of history? Pepys, Proust, Goncharov? But how are people naturally engaging this material? How are they really figuring it out? When Joyce and Proust famously met one evening at a dinner, one complained of stomach pain, and I believe the other complained about money. So even then, the energy is offset—we don't, for instance, hear the one praising Ibsen and solving the puzzle he'd presently faced, nor in the other the heights of Ruskin and the richness of the shade of someone's blush. This is the case because, though books are made of books, these original books, as far back as the Bible, and further still, are made of lives, of days, of context and experience all bound up. The spectacle, eventually, bores everyone.

👁 👁 GUY DEBORD ON THE SOCIETYSPECTACLE: “The spectacle obliterates the boundaries between self and world by crushing the self besieged by the presence-absence of the world and it obliterates the boundaries between true and false by driving all lived truth below the real presence of fraud ensured by the organization of appearance. One who passively accepts his alien daily fate is thus pushed toward a madness that reacts in an illusory way to this fate by resorting to magical techniques. The acceptance and consumption of commodities are at the heart of this pseudo-response to a communication without response. The need to imitate which is felt by the consumer is precisely the infantile need conditioned by all the aspects of his fundamental dispossession. In the terms applied by Gabel to a completely different pathological level, “the abnormal need for representation here compensates for a tortuous feeling of being on the margin of existence.”[28]

[28] *Society of the Spectacle*, 219.

👁 👁 These are the material conditions of just about any reader of Writer's works that I can think of. On the one hand, a sense of total alienation, and on the other, an ingoing stream of messaging and material nearly impossible to parse and seemingly interwoven with our daily existence in a manner equivalent to the family or the fire of the caveman. It's everywhere, and now too the coöptation of what used to be a means of talking back, of articulating the divide "between self and world" obliterated by the spectacle, in the form of every single social media app, and every single prompt by a large corporation to share one's story, one's perspective, simply further obliterates the boundary and disconnects one yet further from a stable sense of who the self is. Writer's method, of publishing fairly seldom, and doing little in terms of press, but not entirely recusing himself from public life, is yet another articulation of a path for writers facing a present wildly more drenched in spectacle than Debord's, and even of the majority of the days of Writer's. In turn, what matters then is the level of care, the level of serious immersion into the act of writing for these people, as demonstrated across Writer's career.

◉ ◉ THE CUTUPS ON THE NOVEL: "In 1959, Gysin wrote : "Writing is 50 years behind painting." He attributed this time lag to the fact that the painter can touch and handle his medium, whereas the writer cannot. The writer does not yet know what words are. He deals with abstractions from the source point of words. Few writers are even trying to establish tactile communication with words. Words are secret untouchable objects, is it not? Superstitious awe of one's medium is crippling, and cripples fall behind. This cultivated distance from the medium also places writing behind film and TV, regardless of content. Unless writing can bring to the page the immediate impact of film, it may well cease to exist as a separate genre. We are no longer living in the 19th century. The omniscient author who can move into the past, the future and the minds of his characters is an outworn device."[29]

[30]

[29] William S. Burroughs' review of Brion Gysin's *The Process.*

[30] Located at 9, rue Gît-le-Coeur, Paris, 6th arr.

👁 👁 Of course there has nearly always been the specter of death hanging over the novel. The novel is dying. The novel is dead. The death of the novel. The death of the author. The birth of the text. Barthes and Writer are optimistic. Writer says as much to the Paris Review, that it "isn't even seriously injured," which is accurate, and it's curious to put oneself in the mind of Burroughs, or Gysin even, when this is being said, and what can thus be taken from it. Abstract Expressionism, when this is written, is being aggressively pushed, though importantly also aggressively *received*, aggressively treated, as the most forward-facing thing in art of any kind in the present from whence this statement comes, and Burroughs' extrapolation of it, in a review, years later, hadn't much moved the needle away from this sense. Music had, slightly, and Burroughs glommed onto punk when it happened as something new, something novel, something different. Writer, even, in *Mao II*, laments the hold novelists once apparently had on the culture, though if this precise day could ever really be said to have existed, it decidedly isn't the moment Writer's probably romanticizing slightly. Ann Radcliffe, Charles Dickens, these were hardly figures deeply interested in what could be called the experimental strain romanticized by Bill Gray in *MII*, nor were Dostoevsky and Tolstoy capable of exerting *too much* effect on their times, and the sad story of Herman Melville probably indicates the widest gulf between the pyrotechnic ambitions and transcendent push of a writer at their absolute prime, and a times that couldn't have been crueler in its disinterest towards the height of his achievement in the novel. And yet, Writer is precisely correct in that interview, as any artist, in any medium, is correct to assert their medium is not dead, never dead, could probably never die, and is *worth* pursuing with the seriousness with which they've come to treat it. This is the problem, of course. The writer is to remain devoted like this, with such energy, and passion, and determination, regardless of the indifference they'll inevitably face. What they can do, then, is strive only to have conversations like this obliquely, throughout and across their work. For Writer, then, if Burroughs and Gysin are right, it means that writers of novels ought to *look*, because the world is looking, at these artworks, these films, that are captivating their public.

👁 👁 In many ways I've grown to believe more in the critical act in writing than any other. I romanticize Ruskin, Hazlitt, and Hickey, for their positions as writers who do not purport to necessarily *create* some grand artwork; they simply wish to observe and interpret their lives. The critic, nevertheless, does seem to be hamstrung by particulars in our present, not least of which is the sprawl billowing out in the aftermath of New Criticism, which begat Structuralism, which begat Post-Structuralism, which began Deconstruction, which begat Critical Theory, which begat Affect Theory, and each of these and lots of others besides might look at *See Spot Run* in dramatically different ways, many ultimately conflicting though their interpreters be Doctors, each as utterly convinced of the urgency and relevance of their interpretation, each as anxious to shed old phrasings and invent new isms despite diminishing general interest and little practical attention to what might result from so reinventing the thing every few years. All the same, I love the critics I love, new and old. I love the graduate students I love. I love the professors I love. I love them, I now see, for much the same reason I've come to love Writer. He's a figure who has committed himself obsessively to something rather unromantic and unbeloved. Perhaps in *Americana* there existed remnants of Beatdom in Writer's practice, but by even the time of *The Names* he's become anything but the archetype of the hip American artist. He's steeped in a language and a mode of viewing the old world for its clashings with the new. Not unlike Schopenhauer's conception of a kind of pure aesthete, who quiets the Will in their fixity on its Representations, both the analyzer and the creator of the text can engage practically anything at all, so long as it speaks to their subjectivity.

👁 👁 GUY DEBORD ON THE SPECTACLE: "The satisfaction which no longer comes from the use of abundant commodities is now sought in the recognition of their value as commodities: the use of commodities becomes sufficient unto itself; the consumer is filled with religious fervor for the sovereign liberty of the commodities. Waves of enthusiasm for a given product, supported and spread by all the media of communication, are thus propagated with lightning speed. A style of dress emerges from a film; a magazine promotes night spots which launch various clothing fads. Just when the mass of commodities slide toward puerility, the puerile itself becomes a special commodity; this is epitomized by the gadget. We can recognize a mystical abandon to the transcendence of the commodity in free gifts, such as key chains which are not bought but are included by advertisers with prestigious purchases, or which flow by exchange in their own sphere. One who collects the key chains which have been manufactured for collection, accumulates the indulgences of the commodity, a glorious sign of his real presence among the faithful. Reified man advertises the proof of his intimacy with the commodity. The fetishism of commodities reaches moments of fervent exaltation similar to the ecstasies of the convulsions and miracles of the old religious fetishism. The only use which remains here is the fundamental use of submission."[31]

[31] *Society of the Spectacle*, 67.

👁 👁 In reading Writer, and in reading him discussing his work, I've become fixated on the moment he quit advertising, and in time became himself. It wasn't so straightforward, though. He says he stopped off at the movies. He says, in turn, this might've influenced his work as a writer more than anything else. He says this, and I begin to reread his work entirely informed by this notion, the Eye, watching, the films again of Antonioni, Godard, Kubrick. New York in the 1970s. If writing truly is 50 years behind painting, it seemed sensible that one of our most prolific and significant writers bypass the conventional practice of literature, engaging first the image and then the word, and what's more engaging the imagistic, symbolic nature of words in turn. In a way, it's not unlike my progressing sense of Warhol, which existed for a time ambiently until suddenly his importance to me was apparent. Writer resonated with writers I admired, and that's what started it. Then I was a student in Chicago, and reading *Mao II*, and reading on the train.

I couldn't immediately go, so there was an interim wherein I finished the novel, and began reading another of Writer's novels, which might've been *Great Jones Street* though my memory is finicky with this stuff and I remember *Great Jones Street* as being a book I read while living in my first apartment, and *Mao II* one I read while living in my second. It could've been something else, but it was apparent from reading the notice on the train that I would go as soon as I could. Viewing artworks in person was up in the air, for me, as far as its effect, but something I've come to associate with Writer was doubtlessly influencing me, this sense of reading the world as dense with potential points of focus from which I might then extract meaning. It could be funny, it could be strange, it could be paranoiac, but when I went to the Art Institute I remember feeling prepared to have a meaningful experience. The museum, because of the range of materials on display, has high ceilings in most every room, and the print itself took over basically the entirety of a wall, facing a glass door exit to the rest of the museum. It wasn't as immediate as this, but my sensation in remembering looking at the print was of inwardly gasping, and sitting slowly on the ground as I looked up at the size of it. It felt like the logic of its size had somehow clicked in my mind; the buildup of reading this book named in honor of this work feels that way, like an actual click in my brain, as if I were now entering a new plane of understanding about perception, and art, and the disparities between the intent and effort of the artist and the response in turn of the audience. I'd seen all these reductions, these distillations of this master reducer, distiller, in Warhol, but my memory of the book gave weight to the image and as I write this I still feel the click, or crunch, of newfound logic applied to a kind of magnitude I'd only previously perceived as small. I repeat it because it, like the time of Writer's formation, proved foundational in my understanding of him. Art was a small thing, and the novel, even, for its grand gestures, was a small thing done in quiet rooms by lonely figures. Somehow, in commingling Bill Gray the writer's plight with terrorism, with large scale weirdness like the mass wedding at Yankee Stadium, a new scale is reached in turn. I am speaking about this more directly than the thing really is, which is of course the trouble with memory. I am repeating the experience because I doubt if I could possibly have spoken to it adequately previously, and memory, too, when presented, as here, as somehow evidentiary of anything in scholarly or academic terms, certainly requires repetition. Memory too as it's applied to the experience of reading, an act which takes place over time, across contexts and moods, but this does not make this dishonest, or fiction. The photograph itself, the lines of brides and grooms and the bright white-clothed minister, the lines in *Metropolis* and the lines in *Koyaanisquatsi*. Writer walked through galleries staring at the Warhol prints, and staring at photographs, and holding a notebook and a pen—*Mao II* is a kind of ekphrastic working, then—even the homeless and the same phrase uttered in Writer's own life. He is transcribing ocular experience but in the willed transported state of one under the program of a shaman. What, when the images are put through the eyeballs of the author, can they then become when rendered in the language of his head? "Here they come, marching into American sunlight. They are grouped in twos, eternal boy-girl, stepping out of the runway beyond the fence in left-center field. The music draws them across the grass, dozens, hundreds, already too many to count. They assemble themselves so tightly, crossing the vast arc of the outfield, that the effect is one of transformation. From a series of linked couples they become one continuous wave, larger all the time, covering open spaces in navy and white."

MII, 3

[32]

[32] *La Semana* N° 298, Argentine magazine (15 July 1982) [Note: this isn't the exact photo Writer's referring to in *Mao II*, but an image from a similar ceremony put on by the Reverend Sun Myung Moon in Argentina.]

👁 👁 I do not, in writing this critique, aim to revivify Writer, as only the reading of Writer might revivify him, hence my tendency to quote, to curate, to assemble—I am figuring something out. If what I can finally offer is a version of subjectivity, or autobiography, but glinted through the works of this person I've never met, whose works I've been considering both highly appliedly and ambiently for over fifteen years, then my only recourse would seem to be a kind of honest, process-based excavating wherein the work is perpetually at hand. I don't want to say, for instance, *here is the skeleton key to this otherwise impenetrable forest of text!* Nor do I wish to simply say *I love it, here's why, so should you*. I am interested in what I might as well consider as the Ruskinian mode of writing on the reaches of architecture amid its ruins, paying attention both to the bricks, their creator, their conception, and one's experience thereabouts. I believe in literature as a means of making sense of one's world, or of omens in one's life. For instance, in weekly sessions in church basements a group of alcoholics consider a story from the Big Book. These to me are higher iterations of the literary critic than will ever exist outside of such context. When the sprawling graffiti of Moonman 157 is considered, then, in *Underworld*, and it proves just outside the grasp, though no less miraculous for this, of any onlooker [this memory is entirely subjective], potentially it's the slight opaqueness of any read description in Ruskin, or any read direction in a manual for a complex new TV set, i.e. there's never an easy 1:1 relationship, and one is always only sifting, inwardly, in the aftermath of language's event for enacted meaning. I wish to say all I might have to say about one author, and much that I might have to say about the role of the critic, using one author.

👁 👁 Writer's implicit thesis, that horrific news coverage, assassinations and assassination attempts, terrorist acts, violent news items and apocalypse culture have replaced literature's temporary grasp on a culture, be it European or American or otherwise, expounded in his BBC *Omnibus* documentary, created in "close collaboration" with Writer, in *Mao II*, in *Libra*, would seem in one sense a dramatic read informed by one writer's need of writing—one thinks of David Markson's annotation of "Bullshit!" in a section attesting to same in *Mao II* on a blog about the books Markson brought to the Strand bookstore near the end of his life—however, more generously, we can also infer a writer's mere relating of their desires for what they do, i.e., *if I'm going to go forward unread, or underread, or misread, then my sense of just what it is I'm doing had better be ironclad, and whether the critics or reading public intend to extend me that generosity, I'm going to investigate just what it is that leads me back to my writer's quiet, my solitude, my near—but only near—Pynchonian reclusion commingled with the littering of my texts across the bookshelves of stores, libraries and any place invested in figuring out the mystery of why any of us should even bother, even try, to approach a form whose most devoted practitioner can only see their efforts as little more significant than the willed self-destruction of walking into a public place and committing violent murder-suicide in one spectacular flourish.* I feel—I hope it's clear—a terrible mess to be writing like this, a great bungle of a human being, not to mention a critic, if you'll permit me. It can be quite frightening to walk at night with no light. "Then he watched *We Were Strangers*. John Garfield is an American revolutionary in Cuba in the 1930s. He plots to assassinate the dictator and blow up his entire Cabinet. Lee knew this was the period of the iron rule of Machado, known as the President of a Thousand Murders. The streets were dark. The house was dark except for the flickering screen. An old scratchy film that carried his dreams. Perfection of rage, perfection of control, the fantasy of night. John Garfield and his recruits dig a tunnel under a cemetery. Lee felt he was in the middle of his own movie. They were running this thing just for him. He didn't have to make. the picture come and go. It happened on its own in the shaky light, with a strand of hair trembling in a corner of the frame. John Garfield dies a hero. He has to die. This is what feeds a revolution."

L, 370

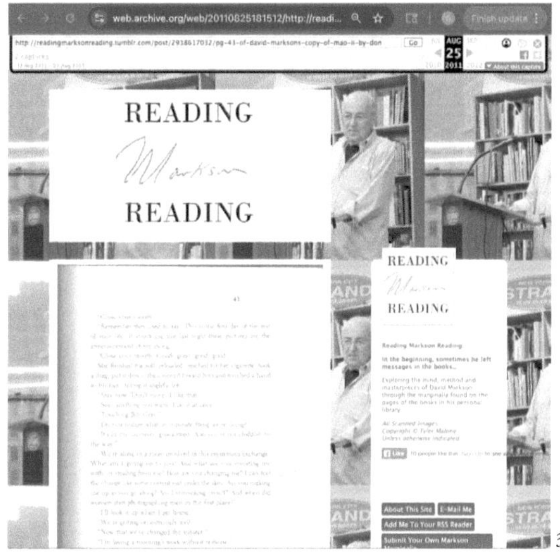

[33]

[33] Screenshot of *Reading Markson Reading.* I'd misremembered that Markson had written this under the novelist-terrorist digression in this conversation, which as you can see, is not so. Markson's annotations to the rest of the book are quite brutal, as most annotations by ambitious contemporaneous writers in the margins of other ambitious contemporaneous writers tend to be.

👁 👁 WRITER ON ZAPRUDER: "Maybe I'm wrong about this but I think the footage comes close to uncovering some secret about the nature of film itself. Film carries something, some mindstream, some myth that may be common to us all. It's as though the experience of film has acquired a kind of independent existence in our consciousness. It's that deeply embedded. Have to get it on film."[34]

[35]

[34] "Don DeLillo: The Word, The Image, and The Gun," Kim Evans, September 27, 1991 BBC 1. The *Times* description of the film: Kim Evan's filmed essay about an American novelist who is obsessed by violent images and what they can do to the soul of a 20th century culture like his, is dazzlingly, nay blindingly, assembled. The camera assumes an adversarial role. It is as much a weapon as the guns that feature so strongly in DeLillo's writing. Therefore, there are two ways of interpreting it when we talk of Evan's scenes being shot. More than one viewing of this film will be necessary for those viewers who simply can't keep up with what DeLillo is thinking, writing and seeing. It takes time to digest statements like "Stalking a victim is a way of organizing one's loneliness, making a network out of it" or "I knew I must extend myself until the molecules parted and I was spliced into the image." In his book *Mao II*, a character says "Keep it simple." Was DeLillo paying attention at the time?"

[35] Screenshot from BBC 1.

[36]

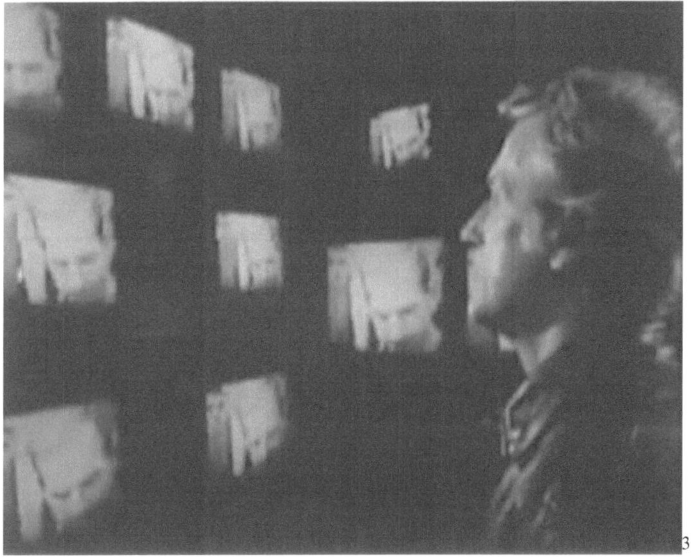
[37]

[36] Ibid.

[37] Ibid.

👁 👁 This documentary feels almost like one of the films of Adam Curtis, a fixation on a particular figure expanding into a worldview that reworks something in the audience. We hear Writer reading from his work. We see Writer sitting, watching Oswald on screen, standing in rooms filled with screens, as above, and looking at real footage of tragic, spectacular events, narrating all the time this fixation on the news, on media, on the ways in which film, when it got put into the viewer's hands, became a kind of compulsion—"It's that deeply embedded. Have to get it on film." (BBC 1) Again the late century's beginning fascination with representations of the world, recordings of the world, repetitions of the world, sometimes even more so than with the events themselves—think of the quite literal granular analysis of filmgrain in the case of JFK, or the more recent *almost* instant analysis of the footage where Jeffrey Epstein was jailed, highlighting that the film had been edited, that chunks of time were lost; it isn't only film critics analyzing the image in this way any longer, it's every average citizen, staring at their screen and trying to extract the mystery they're certain's embedded in it.

👁 👁 WRITER ON SPECTACLE, SYSTEMS, CULTURE: "Q: The word 'system' recurs incessantly in *Cosmopolis*. "I'm helpless in their system, I don't understand it' says a character in the novel. Confronted with the system, you always describe people who fight against it. What are your thoughts now about this idea of 'the system' and its forms of contestation?

DD: Writers must oppose systems. It's important to write against power, corporations, the state, and the whole system of consumption and of debilitating entertainments. And I suppose that in *Underworld* the idea of 'loss› became absolutely central, more pronounced than it was in my earlier work. It›s not something I anticipated but all sorts of destruction peculiar to American culture found their way into this book, from the baseball game that opens the book, with spectators throwing newspapers, to the end of the book, which concludes with nuclear destruction. For a long time, almost ten years, I collected things, objects in dustbins. It was in the 1970s and I didn›t know why I did it. As soon as I saw something abandoned, thrown away, I kept it. And one day I looked at everything I›d accumulated and threw it all out. Two years later I realized how stupid that act had been and I started work on *Underworld*. Be that as it may, I think writers, by nature, must oppose things, oppose whatever power tries to impose on us. You know, in America and in western Europe we live in very wealthy democracies, we can do virtually anything we want, I'm able to write whatever I want to write. But I can't be part of this culture of simulation, in the sense of the culture's absorbing of everything. In doing that it neutralizes anything dangerous, anything that might threaten the consumer society. In *Cosmopolis* Kinski says, «What a culture does is absorb and neutralize its adversaries". If you're a writer who, one way or another, comes to be seen as dangerous, you'll wake up one morning and discover your face on a coffee mug or a t-shirt and you'll have been neutralized."[38]

[38] "A Conversation with Don DeLillo: Has Terrorism Become the World's Main Plot?" *Panic* #1, Nov. 2005, pp. 90-95.

👁 👁 It's a slight reworking, more or less, of Debord. This idea, too, echoes Alain Badiou's sentiments in his "Fifteen Theses on Contemporary Art," in particular number 14, which states: "Since it is sure of its ability to control the entire domain of the visible and the audible via the laws governing commercial circulation and democratic communication, Empire no longer censures anything. All art, and all thought, is ruined when we accept this permission to consume, to communicate and to enjoy. We should become the pitiless censors of ourselves." What does this mean, directly in the context of Writer? That it's no longer enough to seek to merely *express* oneself, because expression in almost all its forms can be coöpted. Like Warhol, every artist is now responsible at least somewhat for the manner in which their works are characterized, the relationship they have with their work in terms of their public, and the degree to which they allow either themselves, or their work, to become coöpted in this way.

👁 👁 Is it only the structures of the modern world that make me ask about the actual worth of criticism? To be so drawn to something, and to so romanticize something, sometimes even higher than I'll romanticize the work that's critiqued, it's like I can't accept it without trying to unpack the numbers, which doesn't lead much of anywhere. The modern world of course is hostile to someone truly immersing themselves in critique, in the manner of a Hazlitt, a Ruskin, a Hickey. They were hostile to these three and others in their times too, it needs be said. But in terms of an individual author, of Writer, what is the aesthetic possibility for a critic who wishes to engage them and convey them to someone willing to read *them*, i.e., the critic, rather than reading Writer himself? This embrace of quotation is hopefully helpful to this end, and constrained quotation, such that these quotations become a kind of sampling, as well as a kind of essay on Writer himself, his works, of course. Updike, for his many flaws, was right in his assertion that the best manner of criticism may be simply quoting the entirety of the work, but short of that—because everyone critiquing everything has to operate, unfortunately, short of that—one's engagement must be on the order of a Wilde, as immersed as they'd be in the writing of a novel, a play—any of it. Is it like a museum curator, working in juxtaposition to affirm the highs and the lows in the trajectories of varied artists? Am I interested rather in creating a kind of unauthorized *Portable Writer*? No, I'm not. If nothing else I can be quite sure that I am not interested in that. It's not even that I want to give someone enough of a whiff, or a skeleton key, to feel that they've henceforward got the works of Writer in the bag, as it were. I realize that I do think of it in terms of a kind of alchemy, as naive as this might be. I feel that if I'm able to *cut* into the body of work in such a way, a mutation might transpire, and the work in this can henceforward be its own entity. This is a dub of Writer. That's what this is. A dub per *King Tubbys Meets Rockers Uptown*. A dub per *My Emily Dickinson*. It is an exercise in changing myself. "We fill pre-existing forms and when we fill them we change them and are changed."[39] "To break the spell I look at a photograph of Borges, a great picture sent to me by the Irish writer Colm Tóibín. The face of Borges against a dark background—Borges fierce, blind, his nostrils gaping, his skin stretched taut, his mouth amazingly vivid; his mouth looks painted; he's like a shaman painted for visions,

[39] BIDART, FRANK. "Pre-Existing Forms: We Fill Them and When We Fill Them We Change Them and Are Changed." *Salmagundi*, no. 188/189 (2015): 613–513. http://www.jstor.org/stable/43942328.

and the whole face has a kind of steely rapture. I've read Borges of course, although not nearly all of it, and I don't know anything about the way he worked—but the photograph shows us a writer who did not waste time at the window or anywhere else. So I've tried to make him my guide out of lethargy and drift, into the otherworld of magic, art, and divination."[40]

[40] Don DeLillo, "The Art of Fiction," No. 135, *The Paris Review*, Fall 1993.

[41]

[41] Portrait of Jorge Luis Borges, by Annemarie Heinrich, 1967. Perhaps it's this photo, though I can't be certain.

👁 👁 The image can become for Writer an infinite source of wisdom and possibility, and in Writer's preoccupations the home video footage of Abraham Zapruder becomes the Proustian knot of familial association and memory from which he's invested in extracting senses and resonant myths from his experience, from our experience. It also, more and more, has become our collective autobiography, these same things stared at and pored over and ogled and obsessed with. We've stared at the same scenes of the second plane flying into the second World Trade Center tower and we've felt the same emotions. Contrarily, the extreme subjectivity of Proust was once the thing to transform ordinary existence into the stuff of mystical wonder, *beauty*, where now the corralling of subjective experience has made it so that writers devoting themselves to small matters, the Knausgards, the Cusks, are praised for zooming in, for distilling slices of life, inventing little, merely recounting in the manner of feeds. Writer, in focusing mostly or wholly on the apparatus of his language, both its visual presence upon the page, its contour, and its interrelatedness with its context, the sentence, can sometimes look like complex machinery in comparison with their small tableaux, but the anchoring elements he's so frequently fixated upon, like Zapruder's film, like the image of the Falling Man, like "24 Hour Psycho," connect us to our larger context and allow this machinery to operate on our consciousness, to see the Proustian wonder in our every day, which just so happens to be showered in blood and violence, terror and cultic mania.

Commission Exhibit 479

42

[42] Black and white copy of frame from "Zapruder film" (z189 from the Zapruder film), showing Presidential limo in Dealey Plaza, CE479 https://commons.wikimedia.org/wiki/File:Black_and_white_copy_of_frame_from_%22Zapruder_film%22_(z189_from_the_Zapruder_film),_showing_Presidential_limo_in_Dealey_Plaza,_CE479.jpg

👁 👁 The presumption that one needs to operate from the perspective of total authority, or even partial authority, in such scholarship, is frankly exhausting and nauseating, i.e. disgusting, rather than becoming nauseated in reaction to or in concurrence with being exhausted. Authority is disgusting and nauseating and exhausting. I don't think it's honest, and I don't think I should behave as if I'm able to prove some point about the work of Writer, because there, really, the only solution would be to direct someone to *read the work*, that's really the only thing the critic, in that context, should do. Not having whatever it would seem to need, not having a Ph.D., for instance, etc. etc., but still wanting to contribute to the general field, to exist within it, still wanting to put my oar in, as it were, the waters of such talk, I'm left a bit astray, afield from where I started, which is really not so far off, since where I started was in stating things about what I hoped for this to do, and part of that was more or less an engagement with such acknowledgements and pronouncements as this. To be inept, then, but *interested*, this would seem to be the state of things for most of us, and certainly was the state of things for those in the graduate program I did attend. To be interested, and inept, then, but not to be setting out any longer to *prove* something, but simply to observe that work, to let it exist as it does, and still too to even point and say look—surely!—look! In writing of DeLillo in this way I am also fearful of obscuring the sense of boredom I can sometimes feel when reading. Not only when reading Writer, though it would be completely inaccurate to say that I have not felt bored while reading Writer. In reading *The Names*, in particular, I can feel quite bored. I don't know what to do with this information necessarily. I feel bored reading quite often. I feel bored when reading *The Names*, I think, because it feels like Writer might be trying to flesh out a novel in the shape that is recognizable to an audience of readers of different, of even avant garde, though also popular, fiction. The aspects in his work that I do not feel compelled by are often elements that fall into this category. This is why his later work has been such a gift. It feels as though *Point Omega* is a distillation of what I've come to love in his earlier work, without any attempt at fleshing things out in works like *The Names*, where a lot of people talk, and there's sometimes a sense of *cleverness*, a quality I absolutely detest in any writer at any time. In *The Silence*, he's showing so much restraint that it almost feels as though he's writing only for me, paring himself down to his essence and attempting to reflect the world as it presently is, having sifted through it all before. The cover on the U.S. edition of *The Silence* is one of my favorite book covers ever, showing simply a lit-up smart phone, potentially a Samsung Galaxy, though I'm not certain. It's a sort of perfect addendum to this thesis that Writer begins in looking, in the eye—and it's worth noting that in reading his work over again with the eye my only focus, I have frequently gotten side-tracked and thought I should write too of *noise* in Writer, of sound; what's more, one potential title for *White Noise* was *Panasonic*, which struck me as the perfect title for such a study, but the eye is what gave me this shape, and thus I won't write again about Writer after this is finished. I should note, too, that I did sift through some of Michael Naas's books on Writer, in the interest of candor, exploring for structure rather than for content, and was briefly totally captivated by his method, wherein the books are quoted from, with their titles listed only as acronyms, and no secondary material to speak of; the cleanliness of the form is truly something to marvel at.

👁 👁 GUY DEBORD ON WRITING: "Writing is its weapon. In writing, language attains its complete independent reality as mediation between consciousnesses. But this independence is identical to the general independence of separate power as the mediation which constitutes society. With writing there appears a consciousness which is no longer carried and transmitted directly among the living: an impersonal memory, the memory of the administration of society. "Writings are the thoughts of the State; archives are its memory" (Novalis)."[43]

[43] *Society of the Spectacle*, (131).

👁 👁 There is a study to be written, not by me, focusing only on the entire *Warren Commission Report* and *Libra*. Per Debord, it would seem to be the perfect text of how to refute the authority, be it of the State, or some other system a writer should find themselves opposed to. That somehow *Libra* got extracted from that forest of bureaucratic handwringing is a marvel. I am however probably not a seer, but a looker—a mere looker—though I don't know if I can notice any difference between these things anymore. We are each of us lookers, starers, and sure, by extension, somehow, seers. Those who merely see. Those who merely look at. These are the people polluting the American landscape, or not polluting it—I do not mean this negatively, I am not interested in negative thinking anymore—but covering it, littering it, though only in this sense referring to their abundance. We are all of us lookers, seers, observers. This is not so bad, though it is difficult to dramatize, to narrativize. Novelists, mostly, repeat the old methods hoping there's enough of the past for the readers to hold on. Some readers find new things, in Writer, or Duras, or Lispector, or Robbe-Grillet, or Trefry, but they are scattered not unlike the lookers who in turn become obsessive terrorists, who also abound in Writer's works, and who might be seen as the ultimate breakage of the looker—the killer, who has gone from stalking to enacting something, has broken through a screen of sorts, if only the thin film outside the den where a tired drunk might skitter in the early twentieth century, to smoke; having broken through, their reality becomes what is looked at, and for the most part in Writer's work this means they must now implode, or if not them, then someone else. But these figures, recounted in the manner they are, by Writer, might also represent Writer's breakage with the control implied by Debord, the opposingly-charged ions any writer navigates in using language, its slippery nature, by offering something back that doesn't waffle, that doesn't skitter, instead it compresses, it hews, it clarifies.

◉ ◉ THE EYE AND THE SPECTACLE IN *FALLING MAN*: "She had several canes to choose from and sometimes, on the off-hours and the rainy days, she walked up the street to the Metropolitan Museum and looked at pictures. She looked at three or four pictures in an hour and a half of looking. She looked at what was unfailing. She liked the big rooms, the old masters, what was unfailing in its grip on the eye and mind, on memory and identity. Then she came home and read. She read and slept." […] "Traffic was barely moving now. There were people shouting up at him, outraged at the spectacle, the puppetry of human desperation, a body's last fleet breath and what it held. It held the gaze of the world, she thought. There was the awful openness of it, something we'd not seen, the single falling figure that trails a collective dread, body come down among us all. And now, she thought, this little theater piece, disturbing enough to stop traffic and send her back into the terminal." […] "He began to think into the day, into the minute. It was being here, alone in time, that made this happen, being away from routine stimulus, all the streaming forms of office discourse. Things seemed still, they seemed clearer to the eye, oddly, in ways he didn't understand. He began to see what he was doing. He noticed things, all the small lost strokes of a day or a minute, how he licked his thumb and used it to lift a bread crumb off the plate and put it idly in his mouth. Only it wasn't so idle anymore. Nothing seemed familiar, being here, in a family again, and he felt strange to himself, or always had, but it was different now because he was watching. […] "Curtis B. could not find his wristwatch. When he found it, finally, in the medicine cabinet, he could not seem to attach it to his wrist. There it was, the watch. He said this gravely. There it was, in my right hand. But the right hand could not seem to find its way to the left wrist. There was a spatial void, or a visual gap, a rift in his field of vision, and it took him some time to make the connection, hand to wrist, pointed end of wristband into buckle. To Curtis this was a moral flaw, a sin of self-betrayal. Once at an earlier session he read a piece he'd written about an event fifty years earlier when he killed a man with a broken bottle in a bar fight, gouging the face and eyes and then severing the jugular. He looked up from the page when he spoke these words: severing the jugular. […] "The skies she retained in memory were dramas of cloud and sea storm, or the electric sheen before summer thunder in the city, always belonging to the energies of sheer weather, of what was out there, air masses, water vapor, westerlies. This was different, a clear sky that carried human terror in those streaking aircraft, first one, then the other, the force of men's intent. He watched with her. Every helpless desperation set against the sky, human voices crying to God and how awful to imagine this, God's name on the tongues of killers and victims both, first one plane and then the other, the one that was nearly cartoon human, with flashing eyes and teeth, the second plane, the south tower."

FM, 12, 32, 64, 94, 133

👁 👁 Here is the weird case of the world catching up with Writer, and Writer regurgitating the world. His 9/11 work, or rather, his post-9/11 work, wherein the paranoia is so lived-in for the general populace it becomes a kind of locus of hostility for Writer, a place ripe for misunderstandings and failed efforts at connection, at art, at communication. In it, a performance artist recreates "The Falling Man" image by AP photographer Richard Drew, depicting a man diving headfirst from one of the burning World Trade Center towers on 9/11. Again, the world catches up with Writer, and Writer, not being interested in merely recreating the contours of the days leading up to, the day of, and the aftermath of 9/11, or any tragedy really, must find some way of engaging the material that feels somehow befitting its weight. Not unlike the mass wedding that opens *Mao II*, or the "Shot Heard 'Round the World" that opens *Underworld*, the reality of the event must somehow get whorled into novelistic submission if it's going to work, as Writer knows the Dickensian 9/11 novels are forthcoming, and even in the case of *Libra* tried to skirt the temptation of writing your conventional JFK assassination novelization; so what is to be done? He creates a fiction, which could feel paltry in the face of such an ugly thing, wherein an artist is assuming the bodily shape of one of the three most affecting images we have from that day, and it infuriates people, and it stirs them, and there's not some great moment of clarity wherein the Mayor declares the performance a masterpiece and everyone holds hands and realizes something. Per Writer, there need only be this *opposition* for the novelist, to systems, to structures, to collective memory, to anything, so long as it is approached at the level of its language and approached in earnest.

👁 👁 Like the movement from a literary work to an adapted film, there's another dimension of Writer's utilizing the eye and the image at the particular point in history he's doing it. This does, in many ways, go beyond Writer, but there is the fundamental, *Ways of Seeing* reality at play in terms of questions on the primacy of language versus the primacy of the eye. Say you're an American on vacation in South America. You've never been, and you drift off while on a hike one day and come upon someone that doesn't speak English. They approach you, and let's say they're carrying a machete. You try speaking with them, and it doesn't work. They approach, a stranger in a strange land, holding a weapon, and they're not saying anything to you. This is not a bind that language is going to help with. You've moved from the comforts of your experience, often guided by language in situations with strangers, to something entirely driven by the eye, by the image, by this innate lizard brain sense of what's a threat, and you've got to figure some way out of it. This sense has been a part of human DNA for a lot longer than language, and certainly thousands of years before text, before reading. Even thinking back to early iterations of what would become the novelistic impulse in mankind, be it Homer, or folk tales, the tendency was usually towards some theatrical accompaniment, be it performance of the contents, musical accompaniment, or qualities in oration. People have had far more time with that as a fictive-literary experience than they have sitting and reading a printed book, so in many ways the modern writer is at a disadvantage so innate potential readers might not even actually register it. In some ways, it seems to contribute to this frequent anxiety around whether or not the novel is a living or a dead thing. On one hand, the high points in its history, the Ann Radcliffes, the Dostoevskys, the Faulkners, the Morrisons, were much closer to small pockets in an ongoing narrative tradition that might've barely noticed. The religious factor, too, complicates matters. The fact that for hundreds of years the primary access most citizens might've had to literary experience was delivered in a church, frequently with accompaniment, with imagery—stained-glass images for windows, large tapestries and paintings, sculptures of Christ on the cross, etc.—and that, what's more, this literary experience was treated as the story of their origin, of God, of the cosmos and the world as we know it, makes the existence of the novel for longer than even one century notable; and endlessly complicates the relationship a reader is going to have with sitting down and staring at black and white symbols on a page, assembling meaning, making connections. A great many writers, both before Writer and after, attempt to deal with this. E.E. Cummings' experimentations with the text itself, down to the letter, to express or evoke new things, new experiences. Gertrude Stein's repetitions, perseverations, language-centric sentences wherein she seemingly burrows endlessly into the thing itself. And with Writer the maximalist tradition is building, Pynchon and Gilbert Sorrentino and John Barth and others jam packing their works with textual fireworks and crazed experimentation to exhume the Joycean impulse and convey the sense of how insane American life was then becoming.

👁 👁 It has become such a commonplace of discourse surrounding the writing of literature in the twenty-first century that it seems an in-built part of the novelist's profession to contemplate the existence or proximity to death of the artform the novelist becomes naturally devoted to. For a sliver of time the novel as an artform held the culture firmly enough in its thrall that to spend any time justifying itself, from practitioners or critics, would've seemed ridiculous, and it's the energy of this thrall that a writer like Writer has certainly carried into his fiction-making. Many writers have abandoned the apparatus of the novel, or the short story—though in the case of Writer the Novel *is* the Thing—absconding for the essay, and varied forms of nonfiction writing that look closer to what Writer has done throughout the bulk of his works than traditional essay writing or memoir. There's something curious, or inspiring, or both, in Writer's case, for his seeming lack of restlessness at least as regards genre. If anything, he's become *more* enmeshed in what it is he does. His most recent work, *The Silence*, feels rather like an "incastellation" of his previous works, or the fashioning of a diamond from the stray coals of a lifetime of preoccupation with terror, technology, names, athletics, media, language, screens, imagery, and more. "Incastellation" refers to the architect, writer, and publisher John Trefry, whose diagrams of "incastellation" will often begin first with, say, a metal pipe, proceeding to a second image, perhaps understandable as the Modernist iteration of art, if the metal pipe on its own was Naturalism, or the original mode of the Romantic Novelist—though incastellation could certainly apply to any artform—wherein the pipe has been slightly crushed, pressed into itself, but not relentlessly so, just so that it's changed *enough*. Incastellation, the final stage, happens when the work has perhaps taken on a mirrored texture, been beaten aggressively, and retains little of its original shape. *The Silence* is an incastellation of the career of Writer, being a distillation of its preoccupations. However, it also represents an incastellation at the level of form, being a "novel," that can't amount to much more than ten thousand words of text, with large, typewriter-style font, double- or triple-spacing, and gigantic margins.

👁 👁 Because he is delimited as a writer mostly of *fiction*, and what's more seems amply compelled to do this in such a way as to be reacting to the world, and giving the world something resonant vis a vis the art experience, we might think of the works of Writer as not dissimilar from the textual sculptures of those, particularly one thinks of Jenny Holzer, whose works exist as small cityscapes, distillations or incastellations of the language of our world, skewed bits of propaganda or anti-propaganda put in the place of massive advertisements; this world, in turn, Writer has left in pursuit of something which will thereafter lead him to writing. He doesn't set out, though, to *become* a novelist, or even a writer, or even anything at all. He goes to the movies. On the one hand, then, the large-scale text fetishization of the advertising boom of the 60s and the 70s, and on the other, the narrativization of the image, the plucking from life, vis a vis Holzer, of scenes which, on their own, might be as meaningless as anything—think of literally any moment in *La Notte*, say—but which, when plucked from context, can become a kind of life, or reality, or anti-life or anti-reality, charged in the same way as the Holzer with not only novelty but the energy of fetishization, often exuding a certain sexuality or certainly at least the desiring state of something mutually agreed upon to hold some power. I never saw in his work the stuff that history has told us writing, and in particular novel-writing, is. I never saw, really, a love of storytelling. Perhaps I never saw this because I wasn't looking for it, but I think it more likely that it wasn't there, or if it was, it was only there insofar as it was somehow required to enact what seemed truly to interest the Writer's spirit behind the text. He seemed to want to hear people talk in staccato ways, like they talked in *Dr. Strangelove*, which is the first and last place my mind goes whenever I read Writer's dialogue. He seemed to want to perseverate over description, to linger over the eye's fetish objects in the world, and though his novels feature characters he seemed to move freely from one set of eyes to another in observation of something else. The names, names like "Nick Shay," e.g., seemed entirely secondary, and more so when compared with the pyrotechnic naming apparatuses at play in his great contemporary, Thomas Pynchon, or the tendency in other contemporaneous fiction writers to really *say* something in naming a character what they're naming them. Even the sculptural nature of language, so abundant in every place else throughout the work, seems entirely flattened when we read "Jack Gladney," "Gary Harkness," or even "Billy Twillig". I'd hazard that as both a reader and a writer Writer doesn't give a shit about character, and in that respect it's difficult to know whether he's simply so determined or we're simply so lucky that critical energies haven't managed to wholly flatten his work from existence—if anything, as is evidenced certainly by *Zero K*, and a late-career genuine experimentation I'd argue rivals, in other terms and by different metrics, the late-career boom period of Philip Roth (relevant particularly because both never fathered children and existed at least in majority part for their work in rather a monastic manner); if anything he's only gotten weirder, and further from the genre conventions the twentieth century and much of the twenty-first has insisted its novelists and writers of fiction follow. This is not to say his work can easily be read as some kind of manifesto per se, for *all* writers of fiction progressing forward; however it does carve out new modes of being for the writing fiction writer, the person actually sitting down and trying to get something figured out.

👁 👁 I have to be wholly honest here if I'm to be of any value, and thus I do have to admit that even though I do feel as though I've found an effective means of viewing the works of this writer, I am also finding myself more glaringly exposed to the ways in which his work is imperfect, which is of course a redundant statement when discussing even those artists—and Writer probably is one—who come closest to approaching a kind of perfection. I do view my life in subjective terms because of the nature of being a person, this sickness we all share and yet for each of us it's slightly skewed. I view the lives of male vaguely heterosexual (I don't actually view things in these terms if I'm honest but in terms of his marriage and my marriage it makes sense) artists in accordance with my own experiences as a male not entirely heterosexual artist, namely as it regards having children, a family, etc. I view these things as nourishing, humanizing forces in my life, and because there can be a tendency towards petri dish microscopic analysis of experience in Writer's works, that is less frequently shot through with the sloppy humanity we might find in certain works by Pynchon (who I do not *love*, mind you; I love DeLillo), here the sloppiness is extracted and the experience can sometimes feel antiseptic. I think this is partly why in this reading/rereading experiment I find myself more drawn to the beginning works of his career, and the late works of his career. Aside from *Libra*, really, and there I think some of the sloppy humanity exudes from the pages of the Warren Report and that hot day in Dallas, works like *The Names*, and even admittedly *Underworld*, just kind of don't hold a candle to those works that seemed to exist as he was *finding* a kind of mastery, but just before it had found its certainty of method.

👁 👁 The novelist-as-terrorist of *Mao II* is too capacious for so particular an act as terrorism, and grows from there, quite immediately, to the hulking frame of *Underworld*, which, perhaps unexpectedly given the book that came before it, almost contains or subsumes this violent figure in the form of Lenny Bruce, tirading on stage in abject glory, but the eye doesn't stop at Bruce, it keeps moving outward, outward from the stadium, from Radio City, from New York itself and into the surrounding dump, a black-plasticky mass spanning impossible miles imagined coated in fog and ambient light—if the terrorist has, then, replaced the novelist, the novelist has somehow exchanged cultural sway and urgency with another authority, a behind-the-scenes look at the killer, the outsider, the rebel. It's a kind of theoretical circling back to Colin Wilson's *The Outsider*. A ticket to the spectacle and a warm seat right next to anyone one might wish, hearing real or imagined commentary from real or imagined personages as a version of the world is torched, or prayed over, or lit up in wondrous colors like the walls of the forest where we imagined Bill Gray hiding.

👁 👁 THE CAMERA EYE IN *MAO II*: "She inserted another roll. She was sure she already had what she'd come for but a hundred times in her life she thought she had the cluster of shots she wanted and then found better work deep in the contact sheets. She liked working past the feeling of this is it. Important to keep going, obliterate the sure thing and come upon a moment of stealthy blessing.

"Do you ask your writers how it feels to be painted dummies?"

"What do you mean?"

"You've got me talking, Brita."

"Anything that's animated I love it."

"You don't care what I say."

"Speak Swahili."

"There's a curious knot that binds novelists and terrorists. In the West we become famous effigies as our books lose the power to shape and influence. Do you ask your writers how they feel about this? Years ago I used to think it was possible for a novelist to alter the inner life of the culture. Now bomb-makers and gunmen have taken that territory. They make raids on human consciousness. What writers used to do before we were all incorporated."

MII, 41

👁 👁 In the novel itself, the author character is being photographed as a part of a larger project not unlike Annie Leibovitz's noted photographs of famous authors—her picture of Robert Penn Warren is truly sublime—or Kevin Killian's "Tagged" project wherein he'd photograph writers and artists holding a sketch Raymond Pettibon drew of a phallus. Here, though, we get their banter, which is significant. We also get a minor treatise from what can probably be understood as a stand-in for Writer, or at least part of Writer, or at least part of Writer at the point in his life when he wrote *Mao II*. It's not an uncommon thing for a writer to bemoan the state of the culture into which they're called to ply their wares. Every writer does it. Some writers, like Mailer or Capote, make a career of it. Mostly their remarks are fine, but seldom as important as the work. In Writer's case, though, given the abundance of characters who engage in terrorist or quasi-terrorist activity or leanings, counterbalanced with his preoccupation with Terror itself, i.e. Spectacle, so redefined around the end of the 20th century, far as we'd moved from Debord et al, he does seem to have tapped into something at the very least explicative of his own modus operandi. What's more, a writer of Writer's nature seemed to resist the temptation prevalent at the wind down of the 20th century and the rise of the 21st to pursue autobiography-in-fiction—not resist it completely, but mostly—and his work is seldom devoted to the subject of fiction-writing itself, or of novels. Art-making, or art itself, is everywhere, as is the making and sharing of visual culture, but for the most part if there's sermonizing on the state of his art it's nicely couched and obfuscated by at least two or three degrees. Even here, really, the novelist can't simply speak, directly, to the reader. The scenario must be spectacularized or subsumed within an art project, simultaneously minimizing and aggrandizing the moment when the treatise comes. I do not know where I fall in the conversation around the weight of the novelist versus the weight of the terrorist, or the cultural import of either, but I do heed it being a potential way into understanding Writer's sense of what he might, in bolder moments, aspire towards. So, if this is, in part, his mission, what is his rejoinder to a culture which might be read as heeding, less and less, the word of the novelist, and more and more heeding the reality of the terrorist. There's a straightforward answer which might serve this book, but I'm not interested solely in acting as though I've found the skeleton key—I haven't, and don't care to (if it isn't clear, I dislike them). I would say it is his language, his devotion to the image as a new kind of sometimes secular, sometimes overtly religious significance, and if I'm honest that might be as far as I'd comfortably go because I do not think Writer concerns himself with much when he's actually sitting down to work. The word, the line, an image, occasionally a figure plucked from real life, or art, or TV. The "concern," it seems to me, is always of necessity smaller. It's easy to feel quite hopeless in the face of the abjection brought about by terrorism. Love, one thinks. Hm, perhaps love, that will fix this. Or the military, sure, perhaps the military will fix this. Or Art, maybe. Maybe Art is the thing. Obviously we can't have a one-to-one solution to something as many-tendrilled, just like we can't have a one-to-one reading of a set of books that quite nearly go every place and concern almost all of modern life, but if a career, or better yet a novelist's career, could be said to respond with anything like adequacy to terrorism, he's at least coming up in the conversation.

👁 👁 I refuse to devote the whole of this monograph to convincing you of the importance of the writer Writer. I can't imagine a dumber use of a life.

👁 👁 GUY DEBORD ON THE NEW WRITING: "Spectacular consumption which preserves congealed past culture, including the recuperated repetition of its negative manifestations, openly becomes in the cultural sector what it is implicitly in its totality: the communication of the incommunicable. The flagrant destruction of language is flatly acknowledged as an officially positive value because the point is to advertise reconciliation with the dominant state of affairs–and here all communication is joyously proclaimed absent. The critical truth of this destruction the real life of modern poetry and art is obviously hidden, since the spectacle, whose function is to make history forgotten within culture, applies, in the pseudo-novelty of its modernist means, the very strategy which constitutes its core. Thus a school of neo-literature, which simply admits that it contemplates the written word for its own sake, can present itself as something new. Furthermore, next to the simple proclamation of the sufficient beauty of the decay of the communicable, the most modern tendency of spectacular culture–and the one most closely linked to the repressive practice of the general organization of society–seeks to remake, by means of "team projects," a complex neo-artistic environment made up of decomposed elements: notably in urbanism's attempts to integrate artistic debris or esthetico- technical hybrids. This is an expression, on the level of spectacular pseudo-culture, of developed capitalism's general project, which aims to recapture the fragmented worker as a "personality well integrated in the group," a tendency described by American sociologists (Riesman, Whyte, etc.). It is the same project everywhere: a restructuring without community."[44]

[44] *Society of the Spectacle*, 192.

👁 👁 There is, I think, an appropriateness to critiques of singular figures and of our romanticization of the individual in our present moment. Again, thinking of the movement of Adam Curtis's films, it seems patently obvious that it is a problem to unquestioningly move into further individualization, to develop no alternative larger structural narratives beyond vitriolic political discourse, sports teams, and at best the smaller structure of the family. This is not, however, what Debord seems to be critiquing or cautioning against. What he seems to be critiquing or cautioning against is art-by-committee, and upholding the social utility of the individual writer, the poet, who remains devoted to their project even in the face of such rejection, such hostility, such indifference while written things that welcome in the group, the larger structure, like film, like podcasting, seem to flourish. This is tricky, obviously, since the writer if they're to be anything more than a Warhol clone had better concern themselves with more than mere navel-gazing, more than mere introspection, and if they're to indicate ways forward they'd better be welcoming in things that surprise even them—it's no accident that one of the best processors of modern experience, in Adam Curtis, is so effective because he spends his time in archives, sifting through the collective language and voice to find a way through individually; and no accident either that his main influence is the individual writer, John Dos Passos; and of course in looking at Writer's work, especially the larger novels (*Underworld's* opening keeps chiming in my head as I write this "He speaks in your voice, American") we can see functioning the utility of a singular presence, a solitary figure, nevertheless interrogating *our* reality, our world, projected onto the perspectives of countless figures who could hardly be mistaken for stand-ins for Writer himself.

◉ ◉ THE SPECTACLE IN *WHITE NOISE* : "The enormous dark mass moved like some death ship in a Norse legend, escorted across the night by armored creatures with spiral wings. We weren't sure how to react. It was a terrible thing to see, so close, so low, packed with chlorides, benzines, phenols, hydrocarbons, or whatever the precise toxic content. But it was also spectacular, part of the grandness of a sweeping event, like the vivid scene in the switching yard or the people trudging across the snowy overpass with children, food, belongings, a tragic army of the dispossessed. Our fear was accompanied by a sense of awe that bordered on the religious. It is surely possible to be awed by the thing that threatens your life, to see it as a cosmic force, so much larger than yourself, more powerful, created by elemental and willful rhythms. This was a death made in the laboratory, defined and measurable, but we thought of it at the time in a simple and primitive way, as some seasonal perversity of the earth like a flood or tornado, something not subject to control. Our helplessness did not seem compatible with the idea of a man-made event.

In the back seat the kids fought for possession of the binoculars."

WN, 123

👁 👁 THE PLAGUE-CLOUD OF JOHN RUSKIN: "So far as the existing evidence, I say, of former literature can be interpreted, the storm-cloud—or more accurately plague-cloud, for it is not always stormy—which I am about to describe to you, never was seen but by now living, or *lately* living eyes. It is not yet twenty years that this—I may well call it, wonderful, cloud has been, in its essence, recognizable. There is no description of it, so far as I have read, by any ancient observer. Neither Homer nor Virgil, neither Aristophanes nor Horace, acknowledge any such clouds among those compelled by Jove. Chaucer has no word of them, nor Dante; Milton none, nor Thomson. In modern times, Scott, Wordsworth and Byron are alike unconscious of them; and the most observant and descriptive of scientific men, De Saussure, is utterly silent concerning them. Taking up the traditions of air from the year before Scott›s death, I am able, by my own constant and close observation, to certify you that in the forty following years (1831 to 1871 approximately—for the phenomena in question came on gradually)—no such clouds as these are, and are now often for months without intermission, were ever seen in the skies of England, France, or Italy."[45]

[45] Ruskin, John, *The Storm-Cloud of the Nineteenth Century: Two Lectures delivered at the London Institution February, 4th and 11th, 1884*. I'm including only Ruskin in response to *White Noise's* characterization of the "Airborne Toxic Event" because A., I'm tired of myself, and B., I simply find it too enticing to directly juxtapose this model of critique with Writer, who of course he could never have read, and yet the two of them intermingle quite well.

👁 👁 THE SPECTACLE IN SCHOPENHAUER: "The essence of shrieking, and consequently its effect upon the onlooker, lies entirely in sound; not in the distortion of the mouth. This phenomenon, which necessarily accompanies shrieking, derives motive and justification only from the sound produced by means of it; then it is permissible and indeed necessary, as characteristic of the action, even though it interferes with beauty. But in plastic art, to which the representation of shrieking is quite foreign and impossible, it would be actual folly to represent the medium of violent shrieking, the distorted mouth, which would disturb all the features and the remainder of the expression; for thus at the sacrifice of many other things the means would be represented, while its end, the shrieking itself, and its effect upon our feelings, would be left out. Nay more, there would be produced the spectacle of a continuous effort without effect, which is always ridiculous, and may really be compared to what happened when some one for a joke stopped the horn of a night watchman with wax while he was asleep, and then awoke him with the cry of fire, and amused himself by watching his vain endeavours to blow the horn. When, on the other hand, the expression of shrieking lies in the province of poetic or histrionic art, it is quite admissible, because it helps to express the truth, *i.e.*, the complete expression of the Idea. Thus it is with poetry, which claims the assistance of the imagination of the reader, in order to enable it to represent things perceptibly."[46]

[46] Schopenhauer, *The World As Will And Idea.*

👁 👁 I picture and visualize the environment of Bucky Wunderlick in *Great Jones Street* quite easily, even if I'm only reading the pages containing lyrics, because I *want* to picture and visualize the environment, because Bucky Wunderlick, the rockstar retiring into reclusion in a slovenly apartment in Manhattan, is so linguistically rich, so lingually compelling, and so reflective of an image we've been showered with since the 60s—the rockstar, the celebrity, in varying states of recovery, on drugs, pursued by skinhead Dog Boys, etc. etc. etc.—on so many magazine covers, in so many TV segments, that the images seem to come flooding naturally. I can hear, too, per Schopenhauer, the sounds of the streets or in the apartment where Wunderlick is staying. It's a novel that seems, alongside *Point Omega*, to embody this completion of an Idea, for what it shows us, and for what it prompts us to see. *GJS* is probably, alongside *Running Dog* and *End Zone*, the most underrated and underdiscussed of Writer's novels, but *GJS* stands out because it seems to connect with these late-period shorter novels he's written since *Underworld*, because he embraces a fragmentation because we're inside of someone's consciousness, and because he seems to be having more fun than he has anywhere else in anything he's written, and though I'm not quoting from it due to circumstances affecting the author (me, not Writer—I gave my copy to the owner of our ice rink, if you remember, in a grave misunderstanding), I'd even say *GJS* seems more fun for both reader and writer alike than *Amazons*.

👁 👁 THE EYE AND THE SOCIETYSPECTACLE IN *GREAT JONES STREET*:

"I slept for a while, very lightly, my surroundings part of the sleep, shaping it in mounds and squares. With my eyes open now I concentrated on various objects within my field of vision. I could barely make out the two candles standing over the sink. The indistinctness of these objects made them seem denser; they were more forcefully present in the near darkness. I slept deeply then, apprehending only myself as object. It was slightly less dark when I woke up, perhaps four in the morning, the room seeming to tremble in the malarial light of that hour. There was no longer any sound of pacing. I turned on my side. Opel was standing in a corner of the room, barefoot, removing her clothes. I lay there watching her, putting her together in my mind as she performed the small acts my eyes could only serialize. I nearly laughed at the way she lost interest in each item of clothing as she took it off, tossing it on the floor or against the legs of a chair, never watching it go, her hands already engaged in the next expert rejection. Her hair was longer now, scattered over one shoulder and deflected at the point of her breast. She had tanned unevenly and her skin was a mass of rash borders and overlapping seasons." [...] "It's too dull to talk about. I only mentioned it in the first place to get my point across. Thingness. If you're interested in things, either take dope or travel to an ancient country. When's the last time you consumed something?"

"The last something I consumed was an animal tranquilizer. That was maybe eleven weeks ago, give or take five or six weeks."

"What was it like?" she said.

"I really don't remember. It was Dodge and me. We were on a hotel roof. We were looking down on the rooftops of the city. Whatever city it was. And I was trying to work out a theory about how you can determine the psychic state of a given society by looking down on its rooftops. Dodge meantime was cackling over this little plastic box he had in his hand."

[...] "In candle-flame she seemed almost an after-image, little left of her ascendancy. Again she is reduced to a point in the middle of the sky. On paper one can find her with the aid of a compass and protractor. She is whisperingly civil, seated between an investment banker and a chummy transvestite, thinking ahead to baggage area and customs. Super-freaks are everywhere, smugglers and global dopers contaminating the air lanes, nitroglycerin concealed in their teeth, unripe opium pods surgically sewn under their eyeballs. Slums and revolution on the 747s. She was in rehearsal for departure now. Ever since Hanes. Hanes had stood in the doorway of my Mediterranean dream." […] "Your power is growing, Bucky. The more time you spend in isolation, the more demands are made on the various media to communicate some relevant words and pictures. We make demands on you not because we're media leeches of whatever media but frankly because proportionate demands are being made on us. People want words and pictures. They want images. Your power grows. The less you say, the more you are. But this is an obvious truism of the industry and I didn't come down here to present my credentials as some kind of theorist or moneychanger in ideas. I'm an on-camera entity. I do my thing and go to black. It's a complicated way to live. Let me tell you in ten words or less what I've got downstairs." […] "The bed was a vast welcoming organism, a sea culture or synthetic plant, enraptured by the object it absorbed. As I headed deeper into mists and old stories, into windy images poised on the rim of sleep, I began to feel that the bed was having a dream and that the dream was me. One candle burned, this light not quite eluding my awareness. I was barely conscious, being dreamed by a preternatural entity, taken for a mind's ride into the mystery of things. It was all a question of control. I was being dreamed-smoked-created. The dream took form as a man asleep in a bed situated in the middle of a room in which a lone candle burned. This was not real but a dream and I was no more than the stale chemical breath of the dreamer. The essential question was one of control."

GJS, 52, 61, 62, 89, 127, 142

👁 👁 What else does one see when one looks in the works of Writer? One sees people, looking, quite often. One sees marriages, and rooms, and people traveling, and killers in cars on highways, and killers riding subway trains for hours. One sees billionaires in limousines, moving, moving, slowly crossing over the city. One sees professors, in robes, sermonizing over Hitler. One sees Hitler, or one wishes to see Hitler, or one aspires to seeing Hitler in the fuhrerbunker, fucking. "The camera is immobile. It does not select. People pass in and out of its viewing field." (*RD*, 226) One sees an elderly couple watch their daughter married off. One sees strangers, standing in rooms, staring, staring, at artworks by Gerhard Richter, Douglas Gordon. One sees films. One sees New York City's late twentieth century evolution. One sees the desert. One sees Greece, the Acropolis. One sees the writer, this aged and reclusive being, surrounded by his simple materials, fielding weird questions strangely.

👁 👁 There are moments in my reading of the Writer's works that are simply lost, and it is not clear what the Reader is to do with this phenomenon. Oftentimes the Critic or the Scholar is presented as an entity like a computer, something that knows things in perpetuity, whose knowledge is either stable or at least steady, because to introduce questioning into the matter might topple the house of cards, as it were. In this case, though, wanting to reflect on the works of a writer and their effect, it seems beneficial to maintain an honesty. To read is often to forget, to simply forget what we have read. We move through scenes, lives, conversations, and if we are analyzing them then we might make notes, and then we will incorporate these notes in some capacity, or comment on them, and then we will move on. The modern Reader especially, whose brain is pulled in so many directions, can find great comfort in the reading of novels, but can also find oneself at a total loss when it comes to summoning back the energies of these novels. It is quite easy to forget that for both the writer and the reader, the creation of this shared experience of the generation of a novel/book and the reading of it is fundamentally creative for both of them. The writer in their expression, the reader in their visualization, their imagining, their hopping from line-to-line, their returning. The reader is not a powerless entity under the spell of the writer. Any work can be read in the manner the reader needs to read it. This entire endeavor, parsing the work of Writer, breaking it up to reflect his own comment in an interview decades back, derived from a need to revisit Writer as a point of influence, not just on myself but on fiction writing in our present world, and on methods of solving the problem of the writing of fiction when so many novels being published can feel utterly D.O.A.

👁 👁 The tendency towards copious amounts of conversations, especially in early Writer, but really throughout, is also symptomatic of this influence of film. For Writer, there is essentially the Godlike voice, which is sometimes first person but most typically third, and there is conversation. Scenes might happen, but these scenes are depicted in such a richness of detail that to get lost in what's happening is almost an impossibility. I do not mean that the details themselves are rich, like in Proust, but that in dealing with the details Writer is particularly concerned with this aspect *of* richness, in terms of the richness of chocolate rather than richness as a good or a bad thing, in assembling his textual edifices. The description, the detail, *is* the thing. Elmore Leonard used to say that the main struggle for him was to simply get his characters talking, and once he'd done that, the book was off and running. For Writer, it's more like 50/50. If characters are talking, they're talking in a manner that has nothing to do with how people communicate in reality. They are talking in Writerspeak. This is neither good nor bad but a fact. You can look even at the quotations provided herein and see the truth of it. If characters are not talking, then the Godlike voice is talking, which is DeLillo himself, sort of, the constructor of the sentences, the maker of the language of the thing, who probably sees himself more as a receptor of it, a receiver, someone looking for le mot juste, than this great fabricator, this great artificer. This balance abounds in modern writing, and certainly modern writing post-Writer. It is a balance forged in film, in TV, where we are either preoccupied with the ways in which the camera is depicting its world, or the talk that's going on within its world. We very seldom move in films from A to B to C, motivated equally at each step as the characters are motivated. Certainly we don't do this in Antonioni, or Godard. In Antonioni, who reverberates through the early novels of Writer like nothing else, but is also abundant in works like *The Body Artist*, where the simple process of a couple in preparation and conversation can become as rich as an intervention, in Antonioni we are witnessing two things: the concoction of Antonioni, *his* fabrication, and his concocting at work upon it. What I mean to say is that his actors are enacting what he's constructed, and the moves around this enterprise, the music, the visual attention paid to particular things, the lighting, the cutting, these are all the efforts of the director. This is why, really, we've never tended as a civilization to treat films as the products of large groups of people. We credit them, sure, but the director, and occasionally the writer, are the thing when it comes to achievement. This basic model, construction/creator, has carried Writer through a career as one of our most ambitious experimenters in fiction, with film opening up paths for his works that wouldn't have been options had he simply followed the paths of a Dostoyevsky, or even of Mailer. Weirdly, and this is where it flips from film, I tend to only get annoyed when reading Writer when people are talking. I want them to stop. I want only his presence, descriptions of what's happening, the weird energy of his prose, to rule the day; but of course you won't sustain a life writing only such things; and gratefully, the conversations are often where humor gets its moment in Writer. The achievement is in being able to bring these inclinations together enough, without simply ignoring the notion that anyone at any point might pick this book up and try to engage with it.

👁 👁 PARAGRAPHING-COLLAGING THE EYES IN CH. 3 OF *AMERICANA*: “People leaned into the traffic. Scouting for cabs.” […] “I was living then in an apartment overlooking gramercy park.” […] “I told her about it and she took it sight unseen.” […] “I can remember that night well, a perfect August night with a warm wind raking the tops of the big oaks, with lawn sprinklers hissing and the silver couples standing near the trees, the men in white dinner jackets and their girls in chiffon and silk, each couple sculpted in the dim light, almost motionless, and the distances between them absolutely right so that the whole scene obeyed and abstract calculus of perspective and tone, as if arranged for the whim of a camera.” *La Notte* […] “Once again, as on so many occasions in my life, I was stirred by the power of the image.” […] “Using fellow students as actors, I made a thirty-minute film for my junior thesis. It was about a man who goes into the desert and buries himself in the sand up to his neck. A bunch of Mexicans come along and sit in a circle around his head. My film instructor, Simmons St. Jean, said it was the most pretentious movie he had ever seen, but that pretentiousness wasn’t necessarily bad.” […] “I wanted to free myself from that montage of speed, guns, torture, rape, orgy and consumer packaging which constitutes the vision of sex in America.” […] “Merry and I explored the desert and I did a lot of filming. I was using a Beaulieu 8mm camera then, the S2008 to be exact, with non-detachable pistol grip, automatic exposure control, an Angenieux zoom lens—all in all, a clever piece of optical mechanics that had set my father back almost seven hundred dollars. The possibilities of film seemed unlimited. Through the camera lens passed the light of a woman’s body. I felt I could do things never done before. A hawk glanced off the sun and I plucked it out of space and placed it in the new era, free of history and death. I made a forty-five-minute film about underwear.” […] “We saw all the new movies and went to a lot of parties.” […] “Each movie we saw was the greatest.” […] “These seductions often took their inspiration from cinema.” […] “The movies were giving difficult meanings to some of the private moments of my life.” […] “Once we saw an old lady in Central Park selling flowers.” […] “It was all there but the soundtrack and I could imagine a series of cuts and slow dissolves working in Merry’s mind.” […] “It made me think and see as I had never done before. In those early days I visualized my mind as a dark room with many doors.” […] “The image of this room was often with me. When I spoke at a meeting I could see the doors opening and closing in my mind and soon I arrived at the point where I could regulated the ebb and flower of light with absolute precision." […] "She was a dark girl with large brown eyes." […] "She looked into the empty ashtray. I put my hand beneath her chin and raised her head, soft eyes shifting, two spoonfuls of tea." […] "I saw her less often and when we were together I was moody and evasive." […] "I saw you on Park Avenue today." […] "You know I'm not seeing anyone." […] "In the darkness that trumpet had a deeper beauty, filling space, leaving time behind, a difficult sound departing and returning, and I did not feel I was in a room with four walls. A note hung at eye level, dim speck on the railroad horizon, then vanished into a long silence shaded by revving bass." […] "You look all scrubbed and fresh." […] "I looked at the TV screen for a moment and then found myself in a chair about a foot away from the set, watching intently. I could not tell what was happening on the screen and it didn't seem to matter. Sitting that close all I could perceive was that meshed effect, those stormy motes, but it drew me in and held me as if I were an integral part of the set, my molecules mating with those millions of dots." […] "Then a commercial came on, one I had seen and heard dozens of times, and I got up quickly and walked around the room, feeling numb and sleazy, the way an awakening man feels when he realizes he's passed out drunk on his host's sofa the night before." […] "My father, whose fantasy life (I suspected) was a curious blend of the dusty vast splendor of longhorn aristocracy and the faultless breeding of English dukedom, viewed this panorama with glacial disdain, one suede elbow resting on the mantelpiece, his stately manor stance, and a putrid cheroot in his mouth—Charles Bickford in a boundary war with some effete sheep rancher." […] "He was much younger than I had expected, a boy of about fifteen, very round and blotchy in appearance, secret eyes peering out of the baby fat, and he had the slightly retarded look of incipient genius—that crowlike scratchy cunning of the city's ragpickers and bottle-savers, those evolutionary masters of survival. The boy looked at me." […] "He was standing on the other side of the avenue near a lightpost, hands cupped to his mouth and the radio tucked into his armpit, calling to me, his bulky figure vanishing and reappearing, a slide presentation, as the cars and buses passed between us." […] "He had fine blue eyes, a disappearing chest and the leisurely belly customary in a man his age." […] "Look, that part of it is beside the point." […] "Look, my last two years in college I took my T-Bird out and back." […] "I'm bringing my camera. We'll get it all on film." […] "She looked almost alluring in Pike's windbreaker, small and dumb and tentative." […] "He hit the table and gazed off into the wings, a look of ineffable disgust on his face." […]

"It's real neat to watch. The ice shines and there's like things going off. Little explosions all over." […] "I was aware of a small movement behind the bar and I knew that one of Zack's shotglass eyes had lifted from the newspaper." […] "Then I smiled at her foolishly and she answered with the unembellished look of a feeble nun who has begged successfully for money and found no hand quite willing to touch her own." […] "Even though I saw her often during those years I was continually surprised by some of the changes in her outlook and personality since our divorce." […] "It was a simple enough job, requiring typing and dictation skills, no more than rudimentary intelligence, and yet it prompted her to explore all the museums and art galleries of the city and to spend most of her vacations, and almost all her money, rummaging through the abbeys and chateaus of Europe, all those tourist bins patrolled by guards who look as though they have just deflowered their own daughters." […] "Meredith's eyes blazed; her arm swept across that vista of stone warriors, philosophers, noblemen and extras." […] "I was looking out on Lennox Gardens." […] "I learned that in an atmosphere of seclusion, intimacy, motel-confessional, no lie is too gaudy, no cliché too familiar, no side-trip of the imagination too dramatically scenic." […] "For a moment I thought of all the old Burtian and Kirkesque characteristics, the clenched emphatic fist, majestic teeth, angry hand brushing the hair, the surprise of a colossal smile, a smile as rich and full as a field of sun-cut Kansas wheat, and then a touch of passionate sadness, low flame in the eyes. Kirk as Van Gogh. Burt as the Birdman of Alcatraz." […] "I carried in the portable TV and we watched a movie for half an hour or so. It was one of those old English films in which people are always promising to meet at Victoria Station the moment the war is over."

A, 29-38, 40-41, 43-47, 49-50, 52, 54-56, 58-60

👁 👁 Looking at it, having just transcribed those sections, after marking them in my copy of the novel, *Americana*, by the Writer, I think about Hunter S. Thompson's approach to transcribing Hemingway to figure out how something like that could be written. I'd sat at the pool, where we'll go in the summer, making notes in that particular chapter of the text, because I'd noticed these moments and these eyes running through it, and liked the idea of, instead of copying in a big chunk like I've done previously, only including the sentences that mentioned these instances of looking, of eyes, in varied ways, and doing it from the physical text, which felt somehow more organic than using an e-book version, which I have, and which I read from too, but I like my copy of *Americana* very much. I don't like it as much as the first edition of *Americana* I've sometimes rented from our library, which features the images of the man with the camera on the cover, and his eye, and which proved a revelatory moment for me when I was considering how to write this text—I have the paperback of the Penguin "Inked" series, where the cover is an amalgam of graffiti—seeing the eye there, seeing the camera there, on this beautiful cream-colored hardcover. I don't know exactly how to characterize the experience of typing out his language. I've done it with other sections here, but here it felt more conscious, assembling this new thing from his language, collaging it together as opposed to one solitary chunk, as I'd said. I believe in this kind of thing, especially as it regards the kind of critique I'm invested in herein trying to enact, and promote, and complete. I think we need to pursue these things, as opposed to mere theoretical handwringing, to keep literature living, and to keep critique living, which to me is too wonderful to simply let die. Postcritique, perhaps, is the word for it, is what people will sometimes call it. I don't mind that term. Autocritique, Autotheory. No. No more theory. Not again. It is, I'm well aware, impossible to wholly imagine the perspective of Writer as he wrote that. We're having trouble with mice, at present. Writer lived in a small, New York apartment when he'd written *Americana*. He'd written it on a typewriter, as I understand it. However, being in a small New York apartment, living cheaply, I'd imagine he had trouble with rats, probably often. I'm lucky to not live in New York City. Writer is maybe the last writer I'm interested in reading who has anything to say about New York City. It is fine to let New York City remain dormant for a time. The mice, though, have an effect on my brain. We had pest control come, and they put these things around the house, poison, in these different boxes, and plugged up various areas. I can't imagine there's much you can do in terms of plugging things up with New York City rats. Writer probably wouldn't have had access to much poison either, or if it was it was pretty crude, as were the traps. I can't imagine what his response to an infestation would've been, but it comforts me to know that he probably endured it while he wrote the things that I just transcribed. I didn't "write" them, exactly. It's foolish to say that. I looked—looked—at them, and transcribed them, that was it. This is, however, a form of analyzing, of critiquing the writing of the Writer, here, if I say it is, and I am, and I do. I detest the skittering of mice. The Writer never had kids, which disconnects me somewhat, because I feel slightly more irked by the presence of the mice as I transcribe anything because I know that I've got my family upstairs, and it's important to take care of them, and this place, and I feel as though I'm failing to do this. He had things he cared for, however, of course he must have. He presently does, and always has. On TV as I write this is an episode of *Game 7*, focusing on a World Series final between the Yankees and the Red Sox. Writer's team, as evidenced by *Underworld*, would've been the Dodgers in his youth, but of course he would've been cheering on the Yankees here, but I can't be sure. The experience of transcribing Writer's words did have a faintly chemical quality to it, very clean, very pored over, very unlike my own tendencies when writing. A word might seemingly leap from itself to the next without a sense of what was coming at all, and I felt stilted, is how I'd characterize it, or stunted, rather. The light flickers, which of course must be the mice.

👁 👁 We cannot, unfortunately, control the things we remember from an author's work. When I think of *Mao II*, I think of the Warhol painting first, and second, I think of Bill Gray, the writer-character in the work, somewhat based on J.D. Salinger's then-recent interactions with the tabloids; of Gray doing this strange ritual of blowing into his keyboard, removing seemingly massive amounts of hair and skin from it. This might be a misremembering, but because I've done the act myself—nothing approaching what he talks about, I'm talking about blowing on a MacBook keyboard, that kind of thing—it's the immediate thing I think of.

👁 👁 MEMORY IN *MAO II*: "Or descriptions just as long and detailed of Bill staying where he is and swallowing. These were his choices, his days and nights. In the solitary life there was a tendency to collect moments that might otherwise blur into the rough jostle, the swing of a body through busy streets and rooms. He lived deeply in these cosmic-odd pauses. They clung to him. He was a sitting industry of farts and belches. This is what he did for a living, sit and hawk, mucus and flatus. He saw himself staring at the hair buried in his typewriter. He leaned above his oval tablets, hearing the grainy cut of the blade. [...] "[Scott] sat at the desk in the workroom now, cleaning the typewriter. He blew on the keys, using a damp rag to lift dust and hair from the felt pad. He opened the drawer to his left, thinking of the next major item on his list, a plan to reorganize reader mail. The drawer held a couple of old wristwatches and some stamps, rubber bands, erasers and foreign coins."

MII, 135, 139

👁 👁 Perhaps, then, it wasn't even Gray doing it? It doesn't seem clear, as things move in and out of the character's consciousness, but it mattered to me in assembling the memory, clearly, that the *novelist* in the book was doing this weird and putrid thing, though even as I look throughout it hardly seems as weird or as putrid as it did in my memory. Weird, certainly, but in my memory that word "putrid" leapt to mind as naturally as anything. And I could see Bill doing it, this photographed, imaged figure in the book. And near to this there's discussion of Mao's using "photographs to announce his return and demonstrate his vitality, to reinspire the revolution," (141) which seems entirely at odds with what Bill Gray is trying to do. He's working on a "long book," and has mapped out the thing with blueprints and the like all over his walls, and it's tempting to think this might be representative of *Underworld*, the book that follows *Mao II*, since the Writer writing about a novelist is always going to bring about the temptation to see the former as the latter, or see aspects of the former *in* the latter, rather, and we know Writer's proclivity for keeping to himself, a sort of reclusion from the world, not quite on the level of Pynchon but certainly second place. So we have a novelist being seen, who does not like being seen, observing Mao—or is Scott observing Mao?—who consciously used his being seen for particular ends, quite successfully, in the context of this novel that makes explicit comparisons with novelists and politically-violent figures, terrorists, and this weird amalgam too of planning out in meticulous detail this massive book, this massive work of communication to the world—*something*—because he feels compelled to do so. Not to be seen, exactly, but for this enactment of language he's responsible for to be seen, and to have some kind of an effect, on the reader. Again I see the clods of dust and skin in my head, the imagined way I've pictured the room, the painting itself and the light in the city at night in other scenes, the scenes at the wedding. These are the images it gives me.

👁 👁 Just now, at 9:58 PM PST, in America, I consider now the reading I've done of Writer's books, and what it is I retain, and what it is I'd like to say of them. I am, in a sense, constrained by it. I am constrained by the heaps of writing already extant on Writer. I am constrained, too, by the considerable limitations put upon the Critic in general. Put upon the Critic in general by history itself, by the history of criticism, of critique, of art, of the novel, of writing and of being a person. To consider Writer, i.e. Don DeLillo, his work itself, and what it has meant for me, or what its proximity to the eyeball has meant to me, I am markedly constrained by these disparate factors. They have sought clarifying power, and clarifying power in language, in category. We have moved from critique to postcritique, yet as with any post- it's never certain whether we've really done so, whether we're not merely treading the same ground in new clothing, etc. etc. I am hobbled, so to speak, by the experience of writing of him. I am worn out by the prospect of writing of him, and yet—and not simply because I've signed a contract, and because I am *attached* to the idea—I am doubly compelled to write of him because of the effect the existence of his body of work has had on me is undeniable. His very existence is something of great power to me, and though the sentiment of it is frankly despicable, quite disgusting, the hope his mere existence offers me is considerable. My father, a learned man, a physician, a nephrologist, who taught me things, and sought to teach me things, and cared about knowledge, disliked "tricks" in literature. He didn't like the feeling that he wasn't understanding the "bit" of an artwork. I can remember, as I began to read more and more, the copy of Writer's *Underworld* on his bookshelf, which I did not read then. I did not read it when I was seventeen years old. This is when I began to read properly. First, I read the usual suspects. Over time, however, I started to gravitate. It is difficult for me, now, to pinpoint which of his books would've been the first. I think—I think—it might've been *White Noise*, but I cannot actually remember the particular edition of the book it would've been. I believe it would've been when I was living as a student at a community and technical college in—in fact the Community and Technical College [of]—Minneapolis. Over the following two years—some of which has thus far been recounted—I began to complete my reading of certain of his books, though not all—and have I now read them all, bearing in mind the temptation to lie in such a situation?—until, when I in fact moved home to my father's home, in Wisconsin, to finish my B.A.

degree in English at the University of Wisconsin-Eau Claire, it began to feel that not only *I* had become ready to read this paperback edition of *Underworld* on my father's bookshelf, *it* had somehow become more ready to be read by me.

👁 👁 THE EYE IN “BAADER-MEINHOF”: “In the painting of the coffins being carried through a large crowd, she didn’t know they were coffins at first. It took her a long moment to see the crowd itself. There was the crowd, mostly an ashy blur with a few figures in the center-right foreground discernible as individuals standing with their backs to the viewer, and then there was a break near the top of the canvas, a pale strip of earth or roadway, and then another mass of people or trees, and it took some time to understand that the three whitish objects near the center of the picture were coffins being carried through the crowd or simply propped on biers.

Here were the bodies of Andreas Baader, Gudrun Ensslin, and a man whose name she could not recall. He had been shot in his cell. Baader had also been shot. Gudrun had been hanged.

She knew that this had happened about a year and a half after Ulrike. Ulrike dead in May, she knew, of 1976.

Two men entered the gallery, followed by a woman with a cane. All three stood before the display of explanatory material, reading.

The painting of the coffins had something else that wasn’t easy to find. She hadn’t found it until the second day, yesterday, and it was striking once she’d found it, and inescapable now—an object at the top of the painting, just left of center, a tree perhaps, in the rough shape of a cross. ”

“BM,” *The New Yorker*, March 24, 2002

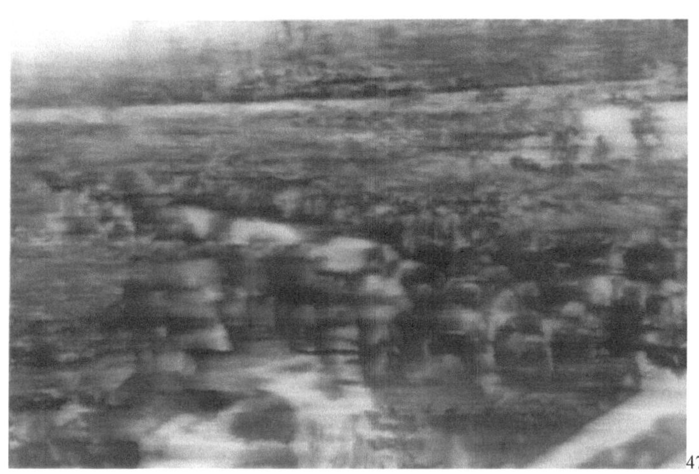
47

[47] "Funeral," by Gerhard Richter, 1988, who said this about the work: "The images are also a farewell, and this in many different ways. In substance: these specific people are dead; then, quite generally: death is farewell per se. Then, in the ideological sense: farewell to a specific doctrine of salvation and, beyond that, farewell to the illusion of being able to change unacceptable living conditions in this conventionally militant way." (*Notes 1989.* In: *Gerhard Richter. Text 1961 to 2007. Writings, Interviews, Letters* . Publisher of the Bookstore Walther König, Cologne, 2008. pp. 221 f.)

👁 👁 I recently finished teaching a course focused on the idea of fragmentation in writing, and fragments as a literary form. We read David Markson, Mary Robison. We watched *Slacker*, we listened to *David Comes to Life*. I knew that I wanted us to read Writer, and as the semester approached I was split between three possibilities, each of which offer new dimensions on the Eye. *White Noise*, which focuses on the Eye of the Consumer, and which had recently been made into a Netflix film by Noah Baumbach. *Point Omega*, which to me represents the best iteration of Late Writer, and which to me is probably the best, purest book of prose he's ever written, focuses on the Eye of the Audience, and "Baader-Meinhof," which does so as well, but in a manner that feels divorced from the viewing in *Point Omega*, the latter of which will be addressed momentarily. "Baader-Meinhof" was first published in the New Yorker in 2002, and thereafter collected in DeLillo's only extant collection of short stories, *The Angel Esmerelda*. Like *Point Omega*, a huge narrative pulse is derived from presenting an individual or individuals in an art museum, looking at art and considering it—it should be noted that this phenomenon happens elsewhere in Writer's oeuvre, the Eye on *Americana*'s hardcover, and the Zapruder sections of *Libra*—and being somehow affected by it. The "Baader-Meinhof" of the title is the Baader-Meinhof gang of terrorists, though it's important that they are, in Writer's story, *depictions* of the terrorists by Gerhard Richter, representations, repetitions of these figures, rather than the terrorist group themselves. Richter's work, who's never named, is on display in sequence in a gallery where a woman, and a man—a stranger to the woman—have gone again and again to view them. It's important because the story is not about terrorism, and because in Richter's rendering the figures are not presented cleanly, they're obscured, blacked and grayed out and fuzzily rendered. This visual strangeness permeates the strangeness of the story, which winds up spinning out into a sort of micro horror movie narrative wherein the female character goes home with the man in the museum, only to become progressively more terrified by him, and him progressively more terrifying, creepy, violent, such that when reading it I always have the sense that the paintings somehow warp this otherwise simple story, a sort of miniature update of *Looking for Mr. Goodbar*, maybe, that now almost feels as though we're watching it on grainy footage, piecing together this mystery, the image of the paintings affecting us just as much as they seem to be affecting these characters.

👁 👁 THE EYE IN *POINT OMEGA*: "The slightest camera movement was a profound shift in space and time but the camera was not moving now. Anthony Perkins is turning his head. It was like whole numbers. The man could count the gradations in the movement of Anthony Perkins' head. Anthony Perkins turns his head in five incremental movements rather than one continuous motion. It was like bricks in a wall, clearly countable, not like the flight of an arrow or a bird. Then again it was not like or unlike anything. Anthony Perkins' head swiveling over time on his long thin neck.

It was only the closest watching that yielded this perception. He found himself undistracted for some minutes by the coming and going of others and he was able to look at the film with the degree of intensity that was required. The nature of the film permitted total concentration and also depended on it. The film's merciless pacing had no meaning without a corresponding watchfulness, the individual whose absolute alertness did not betray what was demanded. He stood and looked. In the time it took for Anthony Perkins to turn his head, there seemed to flow an array of ideas involving science and philosophy and nameless other things, or maybe he was seeing too much. But it was impossible to see too much. The less there was to see, the harder he looked, the more he saw. This was the point. To see what's here, finally to look and to know you're looking, to feel time passing, to be alive to what is happening in the smallest registers of motion."

PO, 5

[48]

[48] Douglas Gordon, *24 Hour Psycho Back and Forth and To and Fro*, 2008, two translucent projection screens showing two 4:3 ratio film projections, viewable from all sides, 24 hours, loop. © Studio lost but found/VG Bild-Kunst, Bonn 2018. *Psycho*, 1960, USA, directed and produced by Alfred Hitchcock, distributed by Paramount Pictures © Universal City Studios. Photo: Rob McKeever.

👁 👁 A figure standing in a museum looking at an artwork. We can take it any way we'd like to. The reality is, it doesn't matter so much the context. *Point Omega* is a spare work, weirdly inflected by *The Names* more than his other books, at least throughout the middle where the bulk of any "narrative" takes place, fairly anonymous figures meeting in homes in the middle of nowhere, having vague conversations about the nature of modernity, its consequences, paranoia, death. It doesn't matter, though, not really. It doesn't matter to me, or to my purposes. I don't read fiction for an approximation of the news. I don't read anything for an approximation of the news. I don't think the point is the event. I don't think events are interesting unless the language being thrown at them or drawn from them is interesting. This is what I mean when I say it doesn't matter so much the context. I meant it is a means to an end. The end, in this case, is the rearticulation in language of an experience of art. The experience of art is an experience of Douglas Gordon's *24 Hour Psycho*, one of those pieces of quasi-conceptual video installation art that gave art more breath around the turn of the twenty-first century. Basically it involved the slowing down of Alfred Hitchcock's *Psycho*, to I believe one frame per second, since the usual film would—I think—project at 24 frames per second, so that it took twenty-four hours for it to play through. Writing that out, of course, I realized my math is, I think, way off, but that's not important. Say a fragment of a frame per second. The film, then, got stretched, distended, and would be projected in such a way that people could walk into this dark room and look at the film in front of the screen or behind the screen, could walk around and sort of live with the film. There was no audio, and though I've never seen the actual projection of the artwork in a gallery as far as I understand this is to the artwork's benefit, and the audio isn't missed. Though I don't feel there's an excess of overlap in the actual work put out by Writer and David Foster Wallace, they were obviously complementary figures, friends, in support of and in admiration of one another, and when reading this opening ekphrast on the artwork I can't help but think of this yearning in Wallace for the transmission of this kind of thing to a reader, a desire for closeness, for a natural means of paying close attention. What seems significant is there are writers of fiction who might have us look at the Family to achieve this, its controversies, its troubles. There are writers, too, who might have us look at something Fucked Up. There are writers who might have us look at New York City, and think about it, and understand just how Meaningful it is. Then there's Writer, who looks at an artwork, in the context of a short, paranoiac novel, a monastic book, a desert book, an imagistic almost haiku exercise in restraint only rivaled by the later *The Silence*, and the artwork is itself a degree of separation from probably the most famous American film ever, with all of its associations, itself a degree of separation from a *novel*, a weird, pulpy book fixated on tabloidy psychology and murder!, and by putting us back inside of this artwork through the eye of his protagonist we can slow way down, and feel time passing, and feel the movement of memory, the assembling of images, the replication of thinking along these lines, perhaps getting us to look twice again at our own lives.

👁 👁 Because I don't see why I wouldn't, I'll say too that my favorite of all of Writer's works is *Point Omega*. The reasons for this are as follows: it represents, as *The Silence* kind of does as well, but not quite, maybe the most direct distillation of Writer's powers at work, his preoccupation with the artist, with the artist in society, with paranoia, with looking, with obsessing and with language. Further, it features what I think of as the warmest articulation of Writer's ideas of the function art can serve in society, in its rendering of Douglas Glover's *24 Hour Psycho*, as a kind of set piece. *Mao II*, I think, attempts to explore the function of the *writer* in society, which is quite different from thinking only about art and about the artist, the latter being more general, and these sections offer a clean, monastic, quasi-religious experience of standing obsessively in a gallery, looking and looking at an artwork on a screen. Finally, and this is different because Writer has published pretty frequently since *PO* arrived, but unfortunately Writer is getting older, and though he continues to push the form I find *PO* just slightly outdoes anything after along the lines I'm interested here: it carves out new space for the novel, for literature, and probably importantly for American literature moving forward into the twenty-first century. It seems to me that literature is at an important point of pivot in its history, when the old ways aren't quite adequate to what the form seems to want to do, and the audience exists in a state of indifference tempered by abundance on the one hand, of books, of images, of ways to spend the days, and paucity on the other, of true newness, novelty, of the spirit of art so present in, say, 1920-1940, for all artforms. I am not, however, saying that these things don't exist, the newness, the novelty, spirit. They exist, and are actually quite plentiful at present. The orbit around only Agustin Fernandez Mallo is wholly sufficient to satisfy anyone bemoaning the death of writing or the novel or any of it. I'm only saying that an indifference is caused by the relative abundance of the material on the one hand, and the relative perception of paucity of these things on the other.

👁 👁 THE ARTWORKS IN *UNDERWORLD*, THE BRUEGHEL AND THE FIELD IN THE DESERT OF LARGE MILITARY AIRPLANES BEING ALTERED. THE MURAL AND THE FILM ITSELF, AND LENNY BRUCE UPON THE STAGE BERATING ALL. THE ROBES AND THE SPIRALING FRENETIC LECTURING OF *WHITE NOISE*, THE CLOUD ITSELF, THE IMAGE REFRACTED THROUGH A REALLY CHARGED AND INFINITELY INTERESTING NEUROTIC SUBURBAN PARANOIA. BOTH THE ARTWORKS OF "BAADER-MEINHOF," I.E. THE RICHTER WORKS, THE SMUDGED AND SMEARED RENDERINGS OF THESE YOUNG, PERHAPS NAIVE, PERHAPS DETESTABLE, PERHAPS IMPORTANT FIGURES—THE FUNERAL—AND THE PEOPLE STARING AT THE ARTWORKS THEMSELVES, THEIR EYES, THEIR OBSERVATIONS OF SAME, OR ONE ANOTHER. DOUGLAS GORDON'S MASTERWORK, RENDERED IN LANGUAGE, RETURNING *PSYCHO* TO ITS ORIGINAL STATE, TO ROBERT BLOCH, THROUGH THE EYES OF A MAN ATTEMPTING TO BEAR WITNESS TO ALL TWENTY-FOUR HOURS OF IT, OBSESSED WITH TRYING AND KNOWING IT ISN'T POSSIBLE. THE ART AND THE IMAGES AND THE SPECTACLES OF EVERY COVER, EVERY EYE, EVERY WARHOL REPRINTED, EVERY HOME VIDEO CAMERA, EVERY SPECTACLE IN *END ZONE*, THE AMERICAN PREOCCUPATION WITH COLLEGE FOOTBALL AS A KIND OF REDEEMING AND PURGATION OF A NATION'S GRIEFS.

👁 👁 What now, in the present, can be the function of critical writing? I have expressed, so far, a real love for this kind of work, a real admiration for it in most respects. Something happened, in recent years, where I suddenly became quite invested in what the critics were doing, became, really, *most* interested in what writers of criticism were doing. It wasn't instant, but it seemed to begin when I started to read, and to consider, Dave Hickey. When I read someone, I no longer only read them. I sort of have to live with them, so to speak, to keep them around me, reading them, listening to them, watching videos of them, saving pictures of them to my phone, reading interviews. I keep them with me. If they ate, or eat, particular things, then I might do the same. I am repeating myself only slightly. I am repeating myself for the sake of this work. In my opinion, and it is only an opinion, reading has, of necessity, grown as culture has grown. Or it ought to have grown. Or it ought to *aspire* to grow. Think, for instance, of the merchandising, and reiterating, of popular films. I was raised not simply to watch *Star Wars*, say, but to eat *Star Wars*, at restaurants, and in gas stations, to read *Star Wars*, in the novels of Timothy Zahn, to wear *Star Wars*, to play *Star Wars*, to listen to *Star Wars*, to watch parodies of *Star Wars*, to know the anecdotes or jokes or voices. I'm certain I'm forgetting things, but this was a part of my cultural training. So, in discovering how I enjoyed Dave Hickey, I kept him around in this way. I watched all I could, in his case mostly lectures, though even an episode of William F. Buckley where he asked Tom Wolfe something completely incomprehensible to me, that Tom Wolfe seemingly completely understood, and answered as if they were old friends. Dave Hickey primarily wrote about visual art, but he wrote in such a way that his writings about art were really writings about absolutely everything, moving from Foucault, to fast food, to Picasso, to television, and everything between. He also, early in life, wrote fiction, developing a strange practice while pursuing (he never finished) a Ph.D. in Linguistics, whereby he could write with symbols, coming up with a means of writing stories I still don't quite understand. From Dave Hickey, I moved to worshiping Pauline Kael, buying what I could, watching what I could, osmotically engaging her and her work where I could. Kael and Hickey are interesting because both, in their way, began as authors of fiction, and over the course of a lifetime turned to criticism. In Kael's case, to film, in Hickey's, to art, while both of them were really writing something far more capacious, more naturally essayistic and expressive, as a kind of alternative to writing fiction, or drama, or memoir, they wrote criticism, because for them it could contain all of it, and probably too because for them it did at times pay the bills, which to me is as admirable a reason to try and figure out the best way in which one might express oneself, if one is being truthful about it. From these, I'd read William Hazlitt, John Ruskin—the latter of whom is particularly important to me, since (and I've written of this somewhere, I'm certain of it) my grandfather left a copy of Ruskin's work that my father had, who gave it to me, which I then lost, which is an ultimate regret of my life, and which I'll seek ambiently for all time, hoping—and began to peruse things like Glossator, as well as watching YouTubers that specialized in a kind of commentary that struck me as particularly brilliant along these lines, namely Horses, whose video on Edgar Allan Poe, in particular, is one of the better works of criticism I've ever encountered. The idea, to me, then, is that critical writing is the writing that can kind of contain all of it. Reviewing, more or less, is a little dead, but that's immaterial. Our present moment is lousy with texts, with artworks, with objects. Accordingly, the human race is overstimulated and overwhelmed. What can be done? Countless things, sure, but the place of the critic seems opportune now in a way it hasn't been before, where critical work can cut through certain layers of shit in modern living that other modes of engagement probably can't quite touch. There is also an elegance, to me, in a kind of ekphrastic position, whereby a writer immerses themselves in something already extant, and seeks to render it anew, or respond to it, or react to it, or rate it in language, not unlike the manner in which Writer has throughout treated the image, be it an extant artwork or something fictitiously observed.

👁 👁 THE WRITER ON METHOD: "There's a zone I aspire to. Finding it is another question. It's a state of automatic writing, and it represents the paradox that's at the center of a writer's consciousness—this writer's anyway. First you look for discipline and control. You want to exercise your will, bend the language your way, bend the world your way. You want to control the flow of impulses, images, words, faces, ideas. But there's a higher place, a secret aspiration. You want to let go. You want to lose yourself in language, become a carrier or messenger. The best moments involve a loss of control. It's a kind of rapture, and it can happen with words and phrases fairly often—completely surprising combinations that make a higher kind of sense, that come to you out of nowhere. But rarely for extended periods, for paragraphs and pages—I think poets must have more access to this state than novelists do."[49]

[49] DeLillo, *Paris Review*.

👁 👁 I think here of the daughter in *White Noise*, and the father watching her, attentively, thinking over this strange dynamic he's now in—a father, a provider, in a context where the air is growing toxic, and everything's falling apart—and he realizes that she's whispering "Toyota Celica" in her sleep. It's possible to look at this as a critique of consumerism. Really, that's probably the most glaring way a person could look at it. The most obvious. It isn't, though, how I naturally seem to experience it in the context of the book. The father in *White Noise* is unlike most of Writer's characters because he seldom so sincerely seemed to want to tackle the question of the American family. This is a natural disinclination for a writer of fiction invested in terror, paranoia, assassination, drugs, money, violence, the future, the ruins of the future, Rock 'n' Roll, football, etc. It's also a natural disinclination for a writer of fiction who never had children. I do think, however, that his ambition to stretch his work in new directions—still today, really—is one thing that can put him far ahead of his contemporaries, and focusing so intently on family life, cut through though it may be with paranoia, Hitler studies, terror, etc., stands out for the ways in which we can see him actively stretching in those directions. Perhaps it's due to the fact that I read Writer as a human American born in 1990, i.e., the notion of critiquing consumerism in varied forms of media is itself as much a part of my pilgrim's progress as consumerism itself, and really overt moves like those in films like *Idiocracy*, though certainly amusing, don't necessarily have the staying power of those things that treat the reality of these varied entities as something as worthwhile to explore in fiction as the Family, City Life, Recovering, War, or Golfers Having Affairs With Each Other's Wives. I don't, e.g., read the sections of *American Psycho* focused on Huey Lewis and the News, Whitney Houston, or Phil Collins and Genesis, and think *Wow, what a biting satire of our celebrity-obsessed era, what a send up of music-obsessives!* To be perfectly candid, I read those sections and instantly want to listen to those musicians, to find ways in which they might be doing things at all conversant with this novel I'm so loving. When I read *Glamorama*, I drank an obscene amount of Diet Coke and ate a lot of Mentos—later seeing what dropping Mentos into bottles of Coca Cola does (creates an incredibly powerful jet of soda twenty or thirty feet into the air) gave me pause, but I survived. This might mean that I am simply more susceptible to product placement than the average human American, but considering the range of relationships I'll have with material like this I don't think that's quite it. With "Toyota Celica," for instance, it is only ever about the phrase. *Toyota Celica*. It's an incredibly pleasant thing to say, even if only inside of your head. It's mellifluous in every respect. It's beautiful. I think, then, of Writer's former career in advertising, and the strange relationship advertising professionals have with the image, with text, with slogans, with the eye, finally, and I'm able to see there's very little critique in the way it's used. It seems, rather, to have wormed its way into Writer's private language—he's letting go, he's following something—sneaking small bits of American experience into the mouths of babes in the same way Joyce paves both *Ulysses* and *Finnegans Wake* with the stuff of his actual Dublin.

👁 👁 THE ZONE IN *WHITE NOISE*: "A random tumble of heads and dangled limbs. In those soft warm faces was a quality of trust so absolute and pure that I did not want to think it might be misplaced. There must be something, somewhere, large and grand and redoubtable enough to justify this shining reliance and implicit belief. A feeling of desperate piety swept over me. It was cosmic in nature, full of yearnings and reachings. It spoke of vast distances, awesome but subtle forces. These sleeping children were like figures in an ad for the Rosicrucians, drawing a powerful beam of light from somewhere off the page. Steffie turned slightly, then muttered something in her sleep. It seemed important that I know what it was. In my current state, bearing the death impression of the Nyodene cloud, I was ready to search anywhere for signs and hints, intimations of odd comfort. I pulled my chair up closer. Her face in pouchy sleep might have been a structure designed solely to protect the eyes, those great, large and apprehensive things, prone to color phases and a darting alertness, to a perception of distress in others. I sat there watching her. Moments later she spoke again. Distinct syllables this time, not some dreamy murmur—but a language not quite of this world. I struggled to understand. I was convinced she was saying something, fitting together units of stable meaning. I watched her face, waited. Ten minutes passed. She uttered two clearly audible words, familiar and elusive at the same time, words that seemed to have a ritual meaning, part of a verbal spell or ecstatic chant.

Toyota Celica.

A long moment passed before I realized this was the name of an automobile. The truth only amazed me more. The utterance was beautiful and mysterious, gold-shot with looming wonder. It was like the name of an ancient power in the sky, tablet-carved in cuneiform. It made me feel that something hovered. But how could this be? A simple brand name, an ordinary car. How could these near-nonsense words, murmured in a child's restless sleep, make me sense a meaning, a presence? She was only repeating some TV voice. Toyota Corolla, Toyota Celica, Toyota Cressida. Supranational names, computer-generated, more or less universally pronounceable. Part of every child's brain noise, the substatic regions too deep to probe. Whatever its source, the utterance struck me with the impact of a moment of splendid transcendence.

I depend on my children for that."

WN, 148

👁 👁 I only want to have failed at precisely the thing I was trying, and not at "solving" Writer's works. I don't read those kinds of books and don't wish to write them. It's not that I find them unnecessary, or a detour from the kind of thing I'm most interested in from an academic/scholarly perspective. It's just that they've never brought me anywhere closer to anything, really. I've tried, with the books on *Finnegans Wake*, but in my opinion the only really worthwhile commentary I've encountered on same are Anthony Burgess', Terence McKenna's, and Roland McHugh's, each of whom do more of a *basking in* than a commentary on, or an elucidation of, *FW*. I also really value John Cage's work with *Finnegans Wake*, who, to finally figure the book out after a lifetime of attempts, at 60 years old, started to *write through* Joyce's novel, producing poems in the form of "mesostics" where he'd spell out different words on different pages, most often J-A-M-E-S J-O-Y-C-E down the center of the page, affixing whatever words were attached to those letters and creating a new poem. That kind of thing, in my opinion, is the future of criticism, the future of scholarship, the *basking in* approach, which, to me, demonstrates to readers ways they might access these things, rather than professing to them what insights they've gleaned. It is also, finally, demonstrably false to assert that Writer's work is *primarily* concerned with the image. It just isn't. It's concerned with many things. I am, however, extremely concerned about writing, about art, about Writer, about the novel, about criticism, and about constraint, and thus the use of lenses is something I view as (hopefully) its own form of not only critique, not only commentary, but of reading, of writing, of basking in and exploring the contours of someone's work. There are obvious preoccupations we can find in Writer's work, but these interest me far less than the Writer himself. Further, they interest me personally less than the particular vantage point from which *I've* arrived at Writer's work, which of course is troublesome, given the purported need for a kind of objectivity in this kind of work, a universality. But we are talking about novels, about fiction, and fiction of a kind that's in fact so subjective that I've frequently had the highly alienating experience of reading commentary on Writer and finding, weirdly, readers are seeing hilarity where I'm seeing something entirely different, something miserable, or seeing "plotting" or the welling-up of historical forces where I am only seeing language. We are, finally, *subjects*. What I have to offer, then, is that subjectivity, though tempered, and rendered through the work, the work and Writer foremost in mind, rather than my subjectivity, to offer *something*, which readers will decide on as they see fit. Critique, to me, is finally and best understood as an art form, a kind of writing that begins with what's in the world, and either burrows into or expands out from that text, or body of work, into something beyond a book review, beyond a yes or a no. History, back through Ruskin and Hazlitt and further, illustrates this pretty clearly and succinctly, that criticism has a purpose and a place and is as complex and wondrous an entity as the novel, the essay, but as we are now in the waning days of the traditional newsprint book review, there's speculation about where the thing can now move.

👁 👁 I watch and I listen to a conversation Michael Naas, an academic, has with other academics at the European Graduate School, a place that I've always romanticized. I realize, again, that I *do* value this work. Naas talks about what prompted him to write two texts on Writer—*Apocalyptic Ruin and Everyday Wonder in Don DeLillo's America* and *Don DeLillo, American Original: Drugs, Weapons, and Other Literary Contraband*—neither of which I've read, and both of which I'll probably not read. I mention them because I mention him, and I mention him and listening to this because he discusses the sense that he arrived at early in his drafting of those texts, that more or less he was not going to consult secondary literature on DeLillo in his writing, and that, thusly, his works would not look conventionally academic, i.e. they wouldn't have a massive works cited section, etc., and that this could function for him as a kind of guiding principle for his work. This notion speaks to me, while Naas himself also speaks to me, as does this ambient sense I've had that both criticism and scholarship have arrived at a kind of standstill. *Immediately*, present critique and present scholarship would seem to say, *it is incumbent upon the critic or scholar to read the entire up-to-date body of secondary work on a given author, one's given subject, so as not to tread upon their ground and so as to generate works which will result in ample citations and improve one's standing, career-wise.* I've experienced this first hand, in fact, when, as a graduate student, I wrote an essay about Herman Melville's novel *Pierre; or, the Ambiguities*, and submitted it to *Leviathan*, probably the most reputable academic journal of Melville scholarship. I knew that in writing my approach I was writing in a highly subjective way, and mining my own experience of Melville's book, and conveying, or attempting to convey, what I'd then been able to extrapolate from the text to this effect. My piece was finally rejected, because I did not care to familiarize myself with what the most contemporary critics and scholars had said in response to the work. There was, however, nothing within my own piece that would've suggested such a thing was at all of interest to me, or at all worthwhile in terms of my approach to Melville. I wrote subjectively, and circuitously, and expressively, trying to offer something as a critic, a scholar, i.e. as someone writing about texts to offer something unique to them, and thus it didn't fit. I don't, I should clarify, think that it was wrong that I was not accepted. The final piece, "The Novelist as Failure, The Language as Failing: A Recursive Reading of Melville's *Pierre*," is hardly a masterpiece of either criticism or scholarship, I know. It was, however, what I had set out to write. In reviewing it now—the piece was eventually published, sans certain academic baubles, at 3AM Magazine—I even cringe a bit at some of it, but in so immersing myself in Melville's book, and in extracting things that meant something to me about being a writer, I'm convinced there was some merit, or worth, in the thing. Is this, then, what I'm pursuing here? I am, certainly, pursuing a kind of subjectivity. However it's a subjectivity that I want refracted, through Writer, and though I've consulted certain sources, most of these have little to do with Writer himself, and focus instead on the Spectacle, or the Image, and are removed from their original context. This was an instance of failure, but in that respect it perhaps represented the perfect response to *Pierre*. This, here, now, is an instance of failure, which doesn't quite have the same ring to it for Writer.

👁 👁 DZIGA VERTOV ON THE EYE: "I'm an eye. A mechanical eye. I, the machine, show you a world the way only I can see it. I free myself for today and forever from human immobility. I'm in constant movement. I approach and pull away from objects. I creep under them. I move alongside a running horse's mouth. I fall and rise with the falling and rising bodies. This is I, the machine, manoeuvring in the chaotic movements, recording one movement after another in the most complex combinations.

Freed from the boundaries of time and space, I co-ordinate any and all points of the universe, wherever I want them to be. My way leads towards the creation of a fresh perception of the world. Thus I explain in a new way the world unknown to you."[50]

50 Vertov, Dziga, 1896–1954. *Kino-Eye : the writings of Dziga Vertov.*

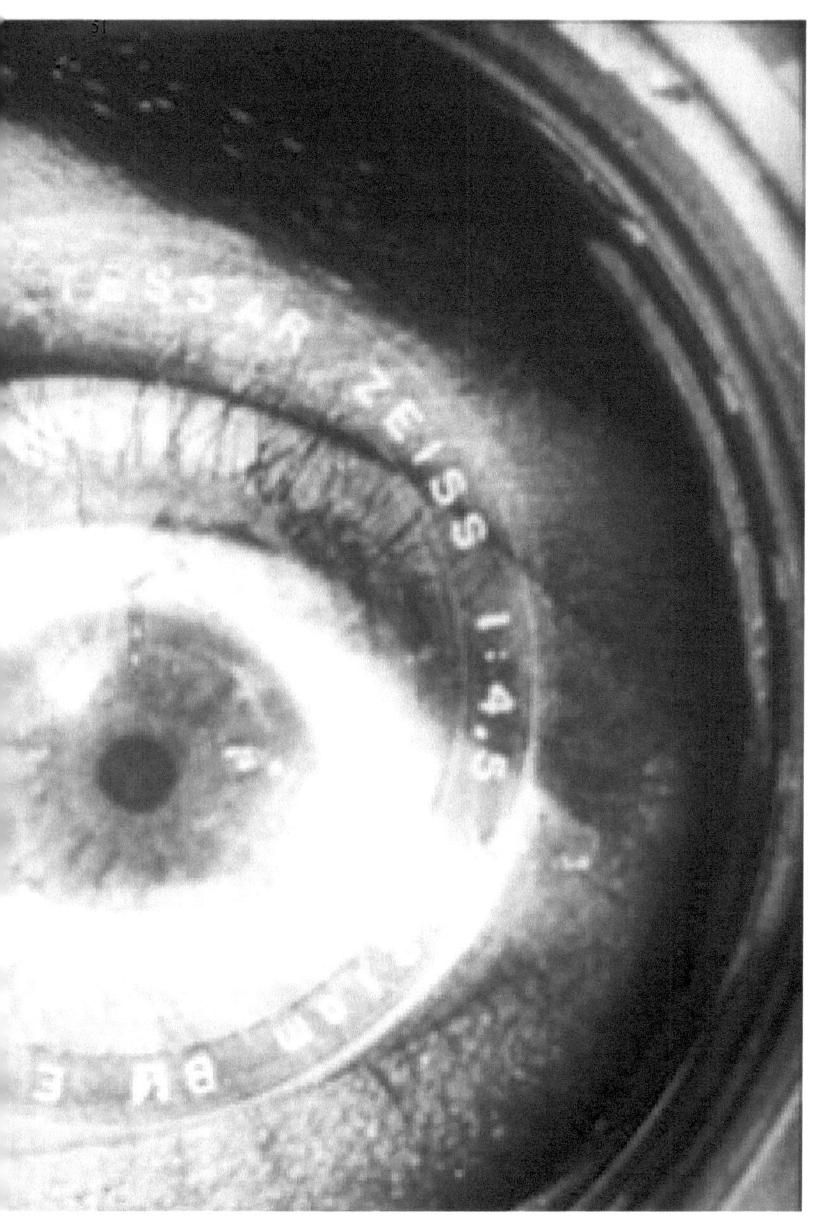

[51] Still from Vertov's *Man with a Movie Camera*.

👁 👁 There is the sense a writer might have when looking at the path before them, and then there is the sense given by Writer, and in the case of the latter, if one is to look only at the work, which is really the only place one ought to look in such a situation, one is to find something similar to what Dziga Vertov is discussing here. This is, at the root level, the only thing a writer might offer anyone, ever, at all. We can say that what they're offering is something else. We can come up with different words for these things. But as Melville's work elucidates, and as Writer's work elucidates when one is truly prepared to become immersed in it, it becomes quite clear one's entire perspective, as best articulated through one's language, is the only thing remotely worthwhile a writer can offer someone else. Otherwise they're doing something different, which might have some worth, but if it's to have the worth that seems to align one with the stuff of history, it ought to be entirely from within the writer's skull. Cocteau said something similar. To listen to one's critics. To focus, in particular, on one's early critics, and to see what they say of one, the negative things in particular, and as one develops further, to hone into those things more and yet more, because they are the only thing that legitimately make you you, speaking of course indirectly about the imaginary figure being critiqued in this circumstance. There is also, of course, this weird dimension of the camera, this weird dimension of the technology, which hopefully through ample quotation thus far has been established. It really is everywhere in Writer's work, this embodiment adjacent to technology. It isn't in some empty critical way. It isn't jeering or satirizing. It is trying, in earnest, to reckon with the world as it is, which seems to be Vertov's perspective, though Vertov's perspective almost feels transhumanist, like something Brian Eno would've said in the 1970s. It has a slight emotional remove, which is a quality in Writer's work I find difficult to talk about. It's difficult to talk of these characteristics, that of a kind of clean, distanced, dispassionate observation, because for me, the phrase that always passes through my head is "a slight emotional remove," which isn't meant in an offensive, reductive manner, a la "I'm so OCD," or something, but merely as an observation, because there's something in Writer's work that seems to beg for such a characterization. It isn't my own perspective. This is something that initially troubled me. As previously acknowledged, it previously troubled me. It troubled me in the sense of his never fathering children, as I'd previously said. It troubled me in terms of our sensibilities never aligning totally perfectly.

How, for instance, could I be influenced by this person, and so inspired by this person, even though I felt these moments of such disjoint with our alignments—who he was and who I was, or who I am and who he is. I am deeply embedded now. I often feel alienated by this experience, which is interesting, since the thing being conveyed by Writer's work, and by other writers' works when I have this sense, is one of alienation. It isn't only writers, either. Of course Kubrick. Kubrick is the biggest in this regard. Kubrick and Writer are extremely similar in this regard. Both of them, often, would say things essentially conveying that they were simply observing the world as they see it, or saying that they didn't know why they did something the way they did, that they just followed it, and that's just where it went. Seeking out contemporaneous reviews of *Americana*, from when it first appeared, per Cocteau, I did find this, which seemed to fit: ""I'm trying to outrun myself," says ex-network executive David Bell (pausing for breath on an Indian reservation) and one must count his effort a success. There is no real identity to be found in this heaping mass of tossed word-salad. There are thickets of hallucinatory whimsy, an infatuation with rhetoric, but hardly a trace of a man."[52] I don't believe it's possible to call a reading of a novel "wrong," given the extreme subjectivity of every reading experience, and really there are ways in which some of what's offered here might not even be deemed offensive to the apparent goals of *Americana*. It's a novel that eludes identity, eludes sure signifiers and stability, much as David Bell himself does over its course, and it feels like it might even be doing so accidentally, as if the goal in writing it was *so* subjective, and so internal, that to try and speak to it now would seem entirely beside the point. I can't, no matter how much I listen to, imagine Writer speaking anything close to wanting to write of "identity," nor of "rhetoric," nor of "traces of men," excepting in the latter's case where portions of *Libra* begin to dissect the ways both the literal assassination halves the persons either victimized or involved, or the ways the Zapruder footage halves both the subjects and the viewers into beings now tethered to its pull. It's the book reviewer's standard snark, and it isn't a horrendous offense or anything, but one can see that if Writer were patrolling the pages, looking for indicators of where to go next, his catalog almost certainly would've suffered.

[52] New York Times Book Review: May 30, 1971 - short notice on *Americana* in "Reader's Report" by Martin Levin.

👁 👁 JOHN BERGER ON THE EYE AND THE WORD: "But there is also another sense in which seeing comes before words. It is seeing which establishes our place in the surrounding world; we explain that world with words, but words can never undo the fact that we are surrounded by it. The relation between what we see and what we know is never settled. Each evening we *see* the sun set. We *know* that the earth is turning away from it. Yet the knowledge, the explanation, never quite fits the sight."[53]

[54]

[53] Berger, John. *Ways of seeing*. British Broadcasting Corporation and Penguin Books, 1977.
[54] Ibid.

👁 👁 When Writer's books are closed, and I am not reading them, and I am not consciously trying to remember the contents of them, there remains, weirdly, *something*. There remains a little voice, though not exactly a voice; it's more as if it's an *un*-voice, or a pre-voice, planted somewhere in the experience of reading Writer's works, and jumbled through nonsense, and nonthought, and images of Writer, and images of Writer's books, and images of interviews with Writer, and quotations, and videos of Writer, and documentaries about Writer, and these things do not get filtered through anything consciously. There are thoughts, of course, about the unconscious, or the subconscious, and the ways in which these things might become affected by only reading something, or watching something, or looking at something, but I can't afford to incorporate that kind of thing at this point in this particular project. There has been too much quotation already, and too much seeking the context or the comforts of the voices of others, and I refuse to do it anymore than I already have—bearing in mind, of course, that this work is being done presently on a page where there still remain pages after, i.e. I'm in the middle of something, and the pages that follow feature further quotes, but as of my writing this now, I won't incorporate anything beyond those already incorporated now. There remains a relationship I have with Writer, and there are these small things throughout the day that will bring him back into my consciousness. Seeing a Toyota Celica and reading its name on its back will almost certainly do it. Seeing particular products, and their juxtaposition, might do it. Hearing particular sentences, or thinking in a vaguely alienlike way about reality, or existence, might do it. Looking up and seeing clouds might do it. These are weird, pre-thought things, I think, having to do with the eye. There is a strange kind of doubled or tripled way in which a writer might access multiple levels, tiers, within the brain as they're working. They can give you multiple experiences in one experience. The book *Cambodia, A Book for People Who Find Television too Slow*, by Bryan Fawcett, or Wayne Koestenbaum's *Hotel Theory*, e.g., these would be two more obvious examples of this phenomenon. Both of these accomplish this feat, of what's probably in line with what Berger's discussing, of the pre-lingual stuff holding weight over the lingual stuff, and the combination of same being really bizarre in its spinning out. In Fawcett's *Cambodia*, this is accomplished by juxtaposing two texts, via footnoting, or sort of splitting the page, and incorporating two narratives or two texts in one book, both of which engage with one another in really curious ways. In *Hotel Theory*, Koestenbaum uses columns, two of which run through every page of the book, prompting one to read part of something simultaneously with something else, leading to a bit of confusion, and an overall experience of reading that reminds me of Writer because it's often a multi-level thing, either in terms of direct structural differences—i.e. the larger text, with something like *Underworld*, and these smaller sections building to something at odds with one's sense of the larger apparatus we might have at any one point—or in terms of the structural stuff happening in language, either in sentences or even individual words, and bigger work being done on the page, more or less, in the construction of a fictional text. All of these elements, are, of course, compounded by what I'd previously indicated, this tendency I have of surrounding myself with anything extratextual to do with writers, artists, and human people I find myself interested in. With Writer, this has frequently bordered on an obsession. At any given moment I probably have hundreds of photos saved, links saved, videos bookmarked, books rented, books in shopping carts online, or books being read to do with Writer.

👁 👁 ANTONIONI ON THE AMERICANS: "I took two trips to America (the first in the spring of 1967 and the second in autumn). I had this idea to do a film here because I wanted to get out of Italy and Europe. Nothing was started in Europe yet, I mean this movement of youth. When I came to America, the first thing that interested me was this sort of reaction to the society as it is now—not just to the society, but to the morality, the mentality, the psychology of old America. I wrote some notes, and when I came back I wanted to know if what I had written down, the intuition, was true or not. My experience taught me that when an intuition is beautiful, it is also true. When I came back I realized that what I had in mind *was* true. I decided on this story when I came to Zabriskie Point. I found that this particular place was exactly what I was looking for. I like to know where the story is placed. I have to see it somewhere to write something. I want a relationship between the characters and the place; I can't separate them from their milieu."[55]

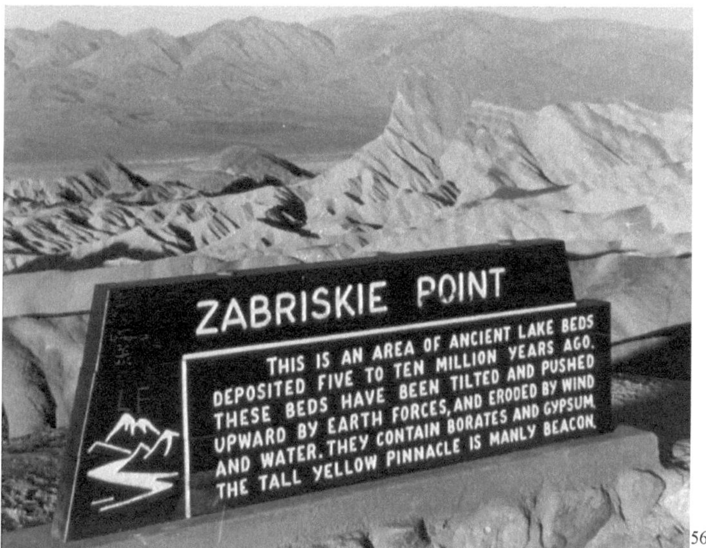

[56]

[55] Antonioni, Michelangelo, Chatman, S. (1997). *The Architecture of Vision: Writings and Interviews on Cinema.*

[56] This is an area of ancient lake beds deposited five to ten million years ago. These beds have been tilted and pushed upward by earth forces, and eroded by wind and water. They contain borates and gypsum. The tall yellow pinnacle is Manly Beacon. Roger469, 10 August 2007, 18:17:00.

👁 👁 *Zabriskie Point* does not feel, really, like a work of Writer's. It does, however, feel almost precisely like the kind of thing David Bell of *Americana* would make if given the opportunity, and some encouragement. This notion of study, too, of a kind of alien's curiosity about the Americans, of trusting one's intuition, and creating a strange, rambling film like *ZP* based on that intuition feels like a subplot of *Americana*, if not something overtly in line with Bell's journey across the American landscape. It is quite easy, I've realized, to write off much of American experience as largely divorced from anything vitally spiritual. Any avenues in, historically, most often had to do with a romanticization of the experience of the American Indian, or of exploration of the early Puritans, witchcraft, and New England. Antonioni, in *ZP*, in his lingering over this space, this movement from the cosmopolis, the cosmopolitan hell, to surreal love in the sprawling desert, to extremity, to violence, is unearthing this strain that seems entirely absent prior to the 1960s, and it's the same vein being mined by Writer, a search for the spiritual tenor, the vibration, underneath America as it presently, and naturally, is, without invention, without imposing things upon the structure like looks far into the past, or the future, or the romanticization of gangs, or cowboys, or detectives, or any of it. Simple American stuff, looking at it, and looking at it, and looking at it, and mining it for its ur-language, its original tongue, its khora, has become the way. The journey, first, to Greece, for *The Names*, seemed to unearth this strain, this new possibility in the work, hinted at in David Bell's particular mania, but cranked up really high and surprising thereafter, finding it in places in American life nobody'd bothered to look, to see.

👁 👁 DEBORD ON CROWDS: "The economic system founded on isolation is a circular production of isolation. The technology is based on isolation, and the technical process isolates in turn. From the automobile to television, all the goods selected by the spectacular system are also its weapons for a constant reinforcement of the conditions of isolation of "lonely crowds." The spectacle constantly rediscovers its own assumptions more concretely." [57]

[58]

[57] Debord, *Society of the Spectacle.*

[58] Fritz Lang, *Metropolis*, 1926. Note: This is not a frame of the film, but a still photograph taken on the set by Horst von Harbou.

◉ ◉ THE CROWDS IN *MAO II:* "The thousands stand and chant. Around them in the world, people ride escalators going up and sneak secret glances at the faces coming down. People dangle teabags over hot water in white cups. Cars run silently on the autobahns, streaks of painted light. People sit at desks and stare at office walls. They smell their shirts and drop them in the hamper. People bind themselves into numbered seats and fly across time zones and high cirrus and deep night, knowing there is something they've forgotten to do.

The future belongs to crowds. [...] "The troops drove the crowd back and the helicopter climbed once more. This time it swept the living away. They fell back from the wind-blast of the rotors and beat their heads and chests.

The voice said, Six hours later, and Karen saw a whole new barrier set up around the site. Cargo containers and double-decker buses. There was a sound track with amplified warnings carrying over the plain that stretched beyond the burial site and there were crowds to the horizon, crowds out to the edge of the long-distance lens.

The helicopter landed with the body in a metal casket, which revolutionary guards carried on their shoulders a short distance to the grave. But then the crowd surged again, weeping men in bloody headbands, and they scaled the barriers and overran the gravesite."

MII, 18, 190-191

👁 👁 It is probably impossible to overstate the significance and accuracy of that statement: *The future belongs to crowds.* Living, as it were, in *Mao II*'s future, the only trouble is the characterization of the crowds themselves, which isn't necessarily prompted or required in the statement itself, which makes it fine, but which, from the perspective of this future, so saturated in the crowd, with every image looking in metaphor precisely like the sprawling chaotic bodies in the bowels in *Metropolis* clawing after something that some figure, some politician, some celebrity, some figure holds, lords over them, screams over them in pinprick accuracy over precisely what it is they need, what he possesses, what they won't be receiving in turn—now, we can understand better the contents of those crowds, the weird juxtaposition which Debord gives, wherein the crowd is there, amassed, ugly, quick to poor judgment, but the crowd is made of these figures who've convinced themselves they are the vital force within it, they are the reason for its existence, they are the shining individual light within the crowd, the genius within the crowd, and they are to be the one that will give it its redemption, its reason for persisting, they will be the way and the truth and the light. A crowd, then, of Jesus Christs, all vying and clawing and justifying and determined to record their acts, to broadcast them, to shout them from the rooftops the moment they've reached the top of the pile, to be heard, to be paid their attention, their allotment, to be seen.

👁 👁 DEBORD ON THE AMERICAN SPECTACLE: Consumable pseudo-cyclical time is spectacular time, both as the time of consumption of images in the narrow sense, and as the image of consumption of time in the broad sense. The time of image-consumption, the medium of all commodities, is inseparably the field where the instruments of the spectacle exert themselves fully, and also their goal, the location and main form of all specific consumption: it is known that the time-saving constantly sought by modern society, whether in the speed of vehicles or in the use of dried soups, is concretely translated for the population of the United States in the fact that the mere contemplation of television occupies it for an average of three to six hours a day. The social image of the consumption of time, in turn, is exclusively dominated by moments of leisure and vacation, moments presented at a distance and desirable by definition, like every spectacular commodity. Here this commodity is explicitly presented as the moment of real life, and the point is to wait for its cyclical return. But even in those very moments reserved for living, it is still the spectacle that is to be seen and reproduced, becoming ever more intense. What was represented as genuine life reveals itself simply as more genuinely spectacular life. [59]

[59] Debord, *Society of the Spectacle*

👁 👁 It is, of course, quite easy, especially for the teenager, to expound upon the nature of American consumption—I don't say this implying Debord was a teenager when he wrote this, nor implying that Debord in his thinking is teenaged, though perhaps there's a bit of truth to this, either that or that there's a certain level of ironic meta-level cognition in the American teenager, most of them anyway, that understands something that's probably pretty obvious, and maybe even a little bit "cringe," but of course none of these components of it make it any less real, or sad, and of course any trace of irony either in American life or commentating on American life is to be treated as suspect, since someone is hiding from something, and it must be rooted out who and what—but, there's nothing really wrong here, and further, though without question Debord is critiquing America, observing something from his perspective that's undeniably negative, the pervasive global spread of this phenomenon indicates probably America was only ahead of the curve. Matthew Specktor, recently, on his Substack *Slow Players*, in writing of the strange American writer Harold Brodkey, offered this: "'We talk mainly about writing and death," DeLillo is quoted as saying. "Those are our twin subjects." When Brodkey asked DeLillo how he might better manage his fear of death (a reasonable question to ask the author of *White Noise*) DeLillo apparently advised him to watch more TV. "It worked so well," Brodkey says, "I went out and bought a huge new television set.'"[60] I referenced this previously because of the warmth of the thinking around TV, and I reference it again both to give proper quotation, and because it expands into the curious predicament no longer only affecting the American writer, but probably all writers; the simultaneous seriousness of their subject matter and their approach, and the logical ridiculousness of their seriousness about same, and the logical ridiculousness of their predicament, i.e. writing fictive books, *opposing* things, treating art with extremity, with seriousness, with the devotion once apportioned only monks, and doing so in a culture largely indifferent, and occasionally hostilely so to their efforts, such that there's no longer any prestige, money, stability, hope, success, position, any of it alotted any of the writers who wish to go all the way; and yet they will, because they have to, and on the flipside of Debord's observation of this spectacular obscenery currently facing all global citizens there seems to be the small hum of Robert Frost's "A Servant to Servants," from 1915:

[60] Specktor, Matthew, Slow Players #26: "Seven Shades of Blue" (Brodkey, DeLillo, etc), July 11, 2025. Substack.

He says the best way out is always through.
And I agree to that, or in so far
As that I can see no way out but through –
Leastways for me – and then they'll be convinced.

👁 👁 DEBORD ON THE SPECTACULAR INDIVIDUAL: The celebrity, the spectacular representation of a living human being, embodies this banality by embodying the image of a possible role. Being a star means specializing in the seemingly lived; the star is the object of identification with the shallow seeming life that has to compensate for the fragmented productive specializations which are actually lived. Celebrities exist to act out various styles of living and viewing society unfettered, free to express themselves globally. They embody the inaccessible result of social labor by dramatizing its by-products magically projected above it as its goal: power and vacations, decision and consumption, which are the beginning and end of an undiscussed process. In one case state power personalizes itself as a pseudo-star; in another a star of consumption gets elected as a pseudo-power over the lived. But just as the activities of the star are not really global, they are not really varied. [61]

[61] Debord, *Society of the Spectacle.*

👁 👁 THE CELEBRITY IN *GREAT JONES STREET*: "The man from ABC had left his card on the table. Although I'd never seen him on television I was able to recall almost every detail of his appearance. He possessed that high gloss common to interchangeable celebrities, to the male secretaries of important female executives, to lawyers with connections in show business. His clothes had seemed extremely tight, equipped with hidden straps, and he hadn't changed expression for the course of his visit. Television. Maybe it was all a study in the art of mummification. The effect of the medium is so evanescent that those who work in its time apparatus feel the need to preserve themselves, delivering their bodies to be lacquered and trussed, sprayed with the rarest of pressurized jellies, all to one end, a release from the perilous context of time. This is their only vanity, to expect to dwell forever in hermetic sub-corridors, free of every ravage, secure as old kings asleep in sodium.

I undressed for the first time in two days, getting into bed naked and weak, unfamiliar with my own body. Fenig began then, taking long and desperate strides, and the soft boy below, Micklewhite's carnival meat, cried four times in the making of a dream."

GJS, 135-136

👁 👁 Everybody now has the weird potential to become a celebrity. Everything becomes equalized. Now the famous might do very little, compared even with Burt Lancaster in *Americana*. Of course, we now know that what these people of the past who became famous for various things *did* is probably negligible. Burt Lancaster didn't do all that much in the grand scheme of human conduct, before or after. Now, though, everything is equalized. In the case of Nathan Apodaca, all it took was skateboarding down the street at sunset, drinking from a jug of Ocean Spray cranberry juice, and singing along to Fleetwood Mac's "Dreams," and suddenly in a burst of light it was all anyone seemed to care about. The celebrity, it seems to me, has grown more polyvalent and weird than even Debord could've anticipated. Even by the 70s, even by the time of *Great Jones Street*, celebrity culture everywhere was very odd. *GJS* is far and away the most fun a person might have, on average, reading Writer. If it were, however, per Frost, simply a way of satirizing, of dancing on top of the absurdity of rockstars, of celebrity culture, it would be long out of print and forgotten. It takes its mythos seriously, and engages with it with such intimacy and abandon to veering vernacular it's like being caught in a wonderful tidal wave that entirely changes one's sense of what novels can be. It doesn't critique, then, from without. It is, probably, useless to critique from without. One cannot go in and come out unchanged, unscathed. Whether writing, painting, making films, making dinner, one must always aspire to having skin in the game, a stake in the matter at hand, if one is to have any influence upon it and to have it meaningfully influence oneself. This is why fiction is the context into which this work is being put, and it's why people will get more animated and aggressive in their tendency to defend or embrace such works when compared with the works of philosophers, of theorists—including, it should be pointed out, among philosophers, and theorists, whose most animated conversations mostly have to do with TV series and films, novels and albums—this is, alas, our lot, our way of making a real sense of the world, and when one is as immersed as Writer is in *GJS*, the thing is affected and inflected by it so wonderfully. There is an argument that would require some veering off, but I'd almost be willing to put forth that *Great Jones Street* is Writer's *Blood Meridian*, almost.

👁 👁 DEBORD ON REALITY: "The images detached from every aspect of life fuse in a common stream in which the unity of this life can no longer be reestablished. Reality considered partially unfolds, in its own general unity, as a pseudo-world apart, an object of mere contemplation. The specialization of images of the world is completed in the world of the autonomous image, where the liar has lied to himself. The spectacle in general, as the concrete inversion of life, is the autonomous movement of the non-living."[62]

[62] Debord, *Society of the Spectacle*.

👁 👁 REALITY IN *COSMOPOLIS (BENNO LEVIN PERSPECTIVE)*: "The pencil I'm writing with is yellow, with the numeral 2. I want to note the tools I'm using, just for the record.

I was always aware of what they said in words or looks. It is what people think they see in another person that makes his reality. If they think he walks at a slant, then he walks at a slant, uncoordinated, because this is his role in the lives around him, and if they say his clothes don't fit, he will learn to be neglectful of his wardrobe as a means of scorning them and inflicting punishment on himself.

I make mind speeches all the time. So do you, only not always. I do it all the time, long speeches to someone I can never identify. But I'm beginning to think it's him. [...] REALITY IN *COSMOPOLIS (ERIC PACKER PERSPECTIVE):* "Heavy trucks went downtown bouncing, headed to the garment district or the meatpacking docks, and nobody saw them. They saw the cockney selling children's books from a cardboard box, making his pitch from his knees. Eric thought they were the same thing, these two, and the old Chinese was the same, doing acupoint massage, and the repair crew passing fiber-optic cable down a manhole from an enormous yellow spool. He thought about the amassments, the material crush, days and nights of bumper to bumper, red light, green light, the fixedness of things, the obsolescences, going mostly unseen. They saw the old man do his therapeutic massage, working a woman's back and temples as she sat on a bench, her face pressed to a raised cushion attached to a makeshift frame. They read the handwritten sign, relief from fatigue and panic. How things persist, the habits of gravity and time, in this new and fluid reality. The cockney from his knees said, I don't ask you where you get your money, don't ask me where I get my books. They stopped and looked, browsing his cardboard box. The old Chinese stood erect, kneading the woman's acupuncture points, thumbing the furrows behind her ears.

Eric saw people stop at the foreign exchange booth on the southeast corner. This prompted him to open the sunroof and stick his head outside, able to get an unobstructed look at the currency prices skimming across the building just ahead. The yen was climbing, still, trading up against the dollar."

C, 56, 82-83

👁 👁 That sentence, that the "specialization of images of the world is completed in the world of the autonomous image, where the liar has lied to himself," seems to me to be an articulation of the practice of the fictive, the snake eating its own tail of the fiction writer, and certainly of Writer, representing the completion, in his finished works, of this circle, which seems to harken to Schopenhauer where Representation might be swapped with "specialization of images of the world," and in the creation of an image, or representation, truly "autonomous," truly self-directed and self-facing, a snake that eats its own tail that perfectly depicts this phenomenon, his work is realized for others to experience this experience, this representation, giving them more relief too from the willing, the desiring, of their days. *Cosmopolis*, modeled on *Ulysses*, about an extremely wealthy man driving across a city to get a haircut, feels like one such realization of this, the creation of a thing unto itself, where the liar, i.e. Writer, has lied to himself. Debord, probably most likely, is talking here of the advertising types, who create images for nefarious, ugly, stupid ends. What's again so wonderful in Writer is he comes from that world, from the mastery of the image for a particular purpose, the mastery over language towards particular ends, from advertising. Now, though, the images are stripped away, leaving only the apparatus of language, and the potential in language to render sight, to render the modern world, to effectively articulate these things for their own sake, to avoid the stink of advertising. When I'd first read *Cosmopolis* I immediately felt that the Eric Packer sections represented the Joycean impulse, and Benno Levin sections the Beckettian impulse. In the former, the tendency seemed to be towards the florid, the ornate, the playful, where in the latter they seemed concerned with monotony, repetition, even ugliness, and an inward turn within oneself. We can't, finally, know whether this is what Writer intended, though it seems at least a useful way to render an autonomous text, to have it comprised of two sections that simultaneously sort of chase one another, commenting on one another without being overt or banal, moving towards, again, the end where the tail gets eaten and we begin again.

[63]

[63] Fol. 279 of Codex Parisinus graecus 2327, a copy (made by Theodoros Pelecanos (Pelekanos) of Corfu in Khandak, Iraklio, Crete in 1478) of a lost manuscript of an early medieval tract which was attributed to Synosius (Synesius) of Cyrene (d. 412).

👁 👁 DEBORD ON THE END: "Where the real world changes into simple images, the simple images become real beings and effective motivations of hypnotic behavior. The spectacle, as a tendency to make one see the world by means of various specialized mediations (it can no longer be grasped directly), naturally finds vision to be the privileged human sense which the sense of touch was for other epochs; the most abstract, the most mystifiable sense corresponds to the generalized abstraction of present-day society. But the spectacle is not identifiable with mere gazing, even combined with hearing. It is that which escapes the activity of men, that which escapes reconsideration and correction by their work. It is the opposite of dialogue. Wherever there is independent representation, the spectacle reconstitutes itself.[64]

[64] Debord, *Society of the Spectacle*.

👁 👁 There is, and it is quite clear now to all, a world inside the world. There are, really, *worlds* inside the world. The world of the image, the world of Writer, is the movement from the twentieth century into now, and in this the recipe for moving beyond it to what, it isn't clear at all. It needn't be clear. Reading novels is a form of hypnotic behavior. One lets oneself become hypnotized, become passive, become receptive. To language, to image, to lines of text on pages. The world being simplified, cleaned, is beyond this palatable, but the world is simpler too than this, the world is always the world of the old and the new, and the beings within the world are both the ancients and the children of the future, of the new world, of the sun, of the solar system. It is always possible to go and to remember the simplicity of living, of life, of the world, of experience. The world of reading novels in *Libra* is the modern world. The world of reading novels in *The Silence* is the simple world, the real world, the world as it actually is. The world of reading novels in *The Names* is the complicated world, the world of ruin, the world of war, of violence. The world of reading novels in *Running Dog* is the world of paranoia, of greeding, of vying so maliciously after so much, all of it relentless and ongoing and never dying. These are only some of the potential worlds, mediated worlds, through which any person might step at any given moment and for any length of time, forever. There was never only looking, of course. There was never only looking through Writer, because the situation called for more than this, but the situation for me called for reduction, for honing my focus, to try and pursue something in Writer to find, and to do this kind of work in a new way, beyond critique, or distant reading, or dissertating. The world it recurs upon itself, in upon itself, and I am only a watcher, someone watching and trying to find something to do with it, and potentially finding something before I can talk, and when I talk the thing takes on new life. If I am partial to any writer's dialogue it is his, it is Writer's. I never cared for dialogue. I cared for it in him because it seemed he was bothered by most of it in turn. Wherever the writer is working at trying to enact something, trying to figure out their work and to do something significant with it, something significant and true, that pushes, that opposes, that does something with the world in language and doesn't let up, the novels being written and the writers writing something are emblematic of this charge, this energy, this attempting to enact something of this spirit, this human spirit, the elusive thing can get sustained, the body artist can enact something of substance pushing back, Writer in turn returning becoming Don DeLillo, the world become quiet and everything done.

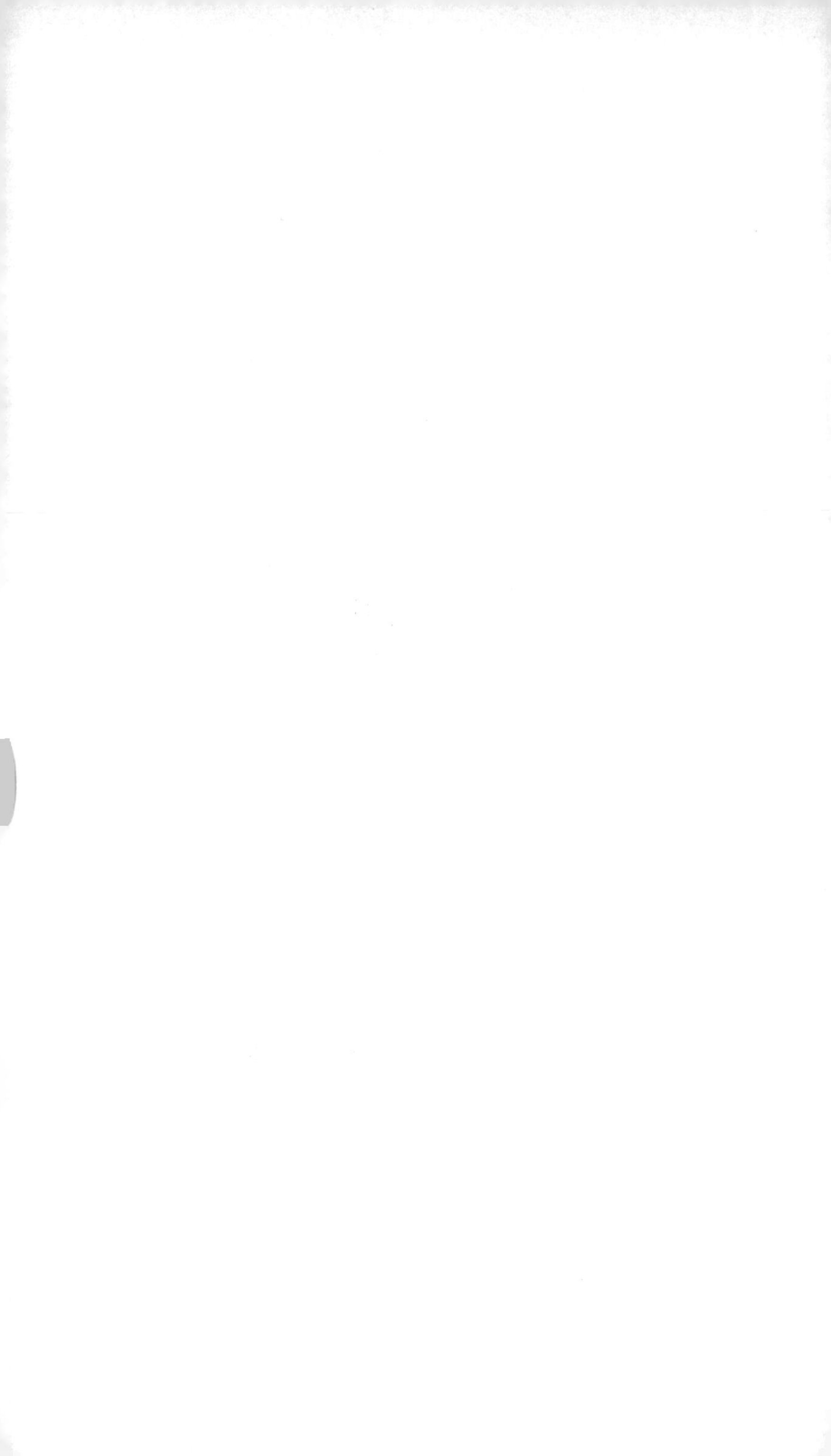